Responding to Alcohol and Other Drug Problems in Child Welfare:
Weaving Together Practice and Policy

Nancy K. Young

Sidney L. Gardner

Kimberly Dennis

Office of Juvenile Justice and
Delinquency Prevention

CWLA Press • Washington, DC

CWLA Press is an imprint of the Child Welfare League of America. The Child Welfare League of America (CWLA) is a privately supported, non-profit, membership-based organization committed to preserving, protecting, and promoting the well-being of all children and their families. Believing that children are our most valuable resource, CWLA, through its membership, advocates for high standards, sound public policies, and quality services for children in need and their families.

CHILD WELFARE LEAGUE OF AMERICA, INC.
440 First Street, NW, Third Floor, Washington, DC 20001-2085
e-mail: books@cwla.org

CURRENT PRINTING (last digit)
10 9 8 7 6 5 4 3 2 1

Cover design by Shelley Furgason

Printed in the United States of America

ISBN # 0–87868-736-X

This project was supported by Grant No. 98-JN-FX-K001 from the Office of Juvenile Justice and Delinquency Prevention, Office of Justice Programs, U.S. Department of Justice.

Points of view or opinions in this document are those of the authors and do not necessarily represent the official position or policies of the U.S. Department of Justice.

Contents

List of Tables

Preface

The epidemic of drug and alcohol abuse that threatens our nation has many economic and social costs, but its cost to families is our greatest national deficit. Increasing numbers of Americans are living on the outskirts of hope and opportunity, with hundreds of thousands of children and adolescents feeling the devastating effects of abuse and neglect, homelessness, violence, and economic erosion. The widespread use of alcohol and other drugs by parents and other family members intensifies these social ills. Families should be on the front line of defense in the nation's war on drugs, but in many cases, alcohol and other drugs have broken through the line. Many children and youth stand unprotected. The child welfare community cannot carry out its mandate to protect children unless there is a dialogue among professionals and caregivers from such disciplines as child welfare, substance abuse prevention and treatment, mental health, juvenile justice, public assistance, and domestic violence. It is through collaboration that effective innovations in policies, programs, and practices evolve.

The Child Welfare League of America is especially grateful for the energy, talent, vision, and commitment of Nancy Young, Sid Gardner, and Kimberley Dennis, the authors of this guidebook. We believe that *Responding to Alcohol and Other Drug Problems in Child Welfare: Weaving Together Practice and Policy* will be a valuable resource to guide the important work that must be done to protect children and strengthen families.

David S. Liederman
CWLA Executive Director

Acknowledgments

This report is based upon the work of an extraordinary group of people who have designed and staffed the innovative model projects that we have summarized. They are the real pioneers in this field, working on behalf of children and families in areas where there are few well-blazed trails. Some of them have taken risks; all of them have made a difference. Among them we would like to single out Toni Moore from Sacramento County and Katherine Wingfield of the CWLA staff.

We would like to offer special thanks to two people without whom this guidebook could never have been completed: Dr. Robert Caulk of Sacramento and Angela Young of Irvine. It was Bob's vision of CWS-AOD links and his deep commitment to doing something about AOD issues that created the Sacramento model. And it has been our niece Angela's generous caring for our two youngest children that made it possible for us to devote the intensive time that this project has required.

We would also like to acknowledge support from the following organizations in the compilation of materials from which this guidebook was developed: The Annie E. Casey Foundation, the Edna McConnell Clark Foundation, the Stuart Foundation, and the Center for Collaboration for Children of California State University, Fullerton.

We are especially grateful to the federal Office of Juvenile Justice and Delinquency Prevention, whose generous support helped to make this publication possible. We extend our deep appreciation to Shay Bilchik, Ellen Shields-Fletcher, and Gina Wood of the Office of Juvenile Justice and Delinquency Prevention, as well as staff from the Office of National Drug Control Policy and the Center for Substance Abuse Prevention of the U.S. Department of Health and Human Services for their continued commitment to improve the quality of life for vulnerable children and their families.

Introduction

Many parents coming into contact with the child welfare system are users and abusers of alcohol and other drugs (AOD), the effects of which impair their parenting skills and threaten the safety of their children. (This guidebook cites estimates of 40 to 80% of all the families in the child welfare system as AOD users/abusers.) In addition to problems with substance abuse, these parents also face difficulties due to their status in the Temporary Assistance for Needy Families (TANF) program (or welfare system), the behavior of their adolescent children, family violence, and mental health issues. As a result, a paradox is driving the future of the child welfare system: decisions and resources *outside* the child welfare system will determine how well that system can serve some of its most important clients—those who are in the caseloads of other agencies, as well as child welfare.

Drawing on the experience of several models of child welfare practice, this guidebook sets forth a policy framework that can assist child welfare agencies in responding to these overlapping problems. Throughout the guidebook, the experience of the Sacramento County Alcohol and Other Drug Treatment Initiative is used as a case study of building bridges between the child welfare and substance abuse treatment systems.

The policy framework focuses on the underlying values of these systems of services, the daily practices of workers in these systems, training, budget issues, outcomes and information systems, and service delivery methods. The guidebook describes several barriers that constrain cooperation between child welfare and AOD treatment agencies, including timing barriers that are summarized as "the four clocks": child welfare deadlines for permanency planning, TANF time limits, the different timetable for AOD treatment and recovery ("one day at a time for the rest of your life"), and the developmental timetables that affect younger children as they bond with adults.

Within daily practice, the most important recommendation—the keystone in the bridge needed between child welfare and substance abuse treatment agencies—is the assessment used by agencies to identify the needs and monitor the treatment of these parents with multiple problems served by multiple systems. We present options for blending assessment instruments that are now administered separately by each set of agencies, resulting in "layered assessments" that make the tasks of line workers more difficult and that force clients to go through repeated, overlapping assessment of their problems. This guidebook also makes a case for screening and assessment of AOD problems in much greater depth within the child welfare system, so that resources from the AOD treatment system can be matched with the known needs of parents.

We describe several models where agencies have been able to develop effective ways of linking child welfare services and AOD treatment and set forth the pros and cons of these models with a matrix that summarizes all nine models. The text reviews innovative practices in both the child welfare and substance abuse treatment fields, including changes in approaches to families, in interviewing techniques, in community partnerships, and in using treatment outcomes to determine which programs are most effective for which clients.

The guidebook reviews evidence of the demonstrated effectiveness of treatment for parents in the child welfare system, and makes a case that treatment has a significant payoff in costs that can be avoided if only a portion of the parents are able to reunify with their children. The report discusses the differences between parents who can be treated successfully after one episode of treatment, those who return for additional treatment episodes and eventually succeed, and those who do not succeed in treatment.

Because of the co-occurrence of AOD problems with clients affected by welfare reform, juvenile justice, family violence, and mental health, the report asserts that the CWS-AOD linkage is not enough, and goes on to describe models of stronger connections between child welfare clients and these other populations.

We draw nine lessons from the models, outline innovative practices, and present our recommendations based on these lessons. Addressing values issues that underlie policy disagreements is a major recommendation, along with active involvement of line workers whose support is essential to the success of innovation at front lines of the organization. The recommendations include urging use of several policy tools that are available to communities working in collaboratives, including resource mapping, budget analysis, annual spending inventories, a collaborative values inventory, and data matching to identify overlapping clients. Recommendations also call for the development of a "theory of resources" to ensure that pilot projects can expand beyond their initial areas of operation to tap the substantial funding for AOD treatment already available to communities.

In closing, the guidebook proposes several federal responses, including upgrading data collection, supporting blended funding experiments, and capitalizing on a requirement for a report to Congress from the Department of Health and Human Services on CWS-AOD issues in the new Adoption and Safe Families Act of 1997.

Appendix A includes a questionnaire used for assessing a community or collaborative's relative consensus on values concerning alcohol and other drugs, and Appendix B includes a dialogue among community participants, which illustrates some of the practice and policy choices discussed in the report. Appendix C lists members of the Review Panel, and Appendix D is the CWLA's Chemical Dependency and Child Welfare Task Force.

In conclusion, the report recalls the strong recommendations of the 1992 report of the North American Commission on Chemical Dependency and Child Welfare, which called for challenging the policies and practices of national and state efforts—and called for continued efforts to keep such challenges alive, building on the lessons of the model projects described in the report.

1

Facing the Problem

Introduction

Many parents coming into contact with the child welfare system are users and abusers of alcohol and other drugs (AOD), the effects of which can impair their parenting skills and threaten the safety of their children. Every child welfare agency in the nation has struggled with AOD problems among its caseload, and many have attempted to build more effective bridges between child welfare services (CWS) and AOD abuse treatment services. Those agencies that have been most active in addressing substance abuse have recognized that it is not a "stand-alone" issue, but rather is linked with delinquency, family violence,

---

Organization of the Guidebook

Chapter 1 describes the overall framework in which AOD-CWS policy issues are currently addressed, summarizing the underlying values and circumstances that affect practice and policy regarding the connection between child welfare and AOD services. Chapter 2 presents several models of CWS-AOD connections, as well as recent innovations within the CWS field. Chapter 3 examines the lessons emerging from the models and innovative practices, and Chapter 4 describes AOD treatment and special issues for children. Chapter 5 defines the role of assessment in linking CWS and AOD services. In Chapter 6, we discuss the need for child welfare reform efforts to understand the roles of other service systems in addressing AOD-related problems. In the final chapter, we present recommendations for strengthening practices and refining policy. Throughout the guidebook, the experience from Sacramento County, California, is used as a case study of the issues and is highlighted in the report.

---

welfare reform, mental health, and the need for a stronger community role in supporting families. This guidebook focuses on understanding and improving approaches to AOD problems among child welfare clients, but also calls for a recognition of the several other problems beyond substance abuse that afflict many families.

Evidence drawn from numerous studies across the nation produces estimates that 40 to 80% of families in the child welfare system have problems with alcohol and other drugs and that those problems are connected with the abuse and neglect experienced by their children. Children are affected by their parents' alcohol and drug use in several ways, as illustrated in the chart on the following page. While prenatal exposure has received a great deal of attention in recent years, Table 1 shows that many more children can also be exposed through the behavior of their parents and through the environment in which they grow up. The underlying premise of this guidebook is that *all* of these forms of exposure to children are harmful and that child welfare agencies and AOD treatment agencies must increasingly work together to reduce this harm.

The Scope of the Problem

Problems related to the use of alcohol and other drugs impact the child welfare system in a number of ways—by increasing CPS caseloads, contributing to the number of children entering foster care, and interfering with the ability of families on welfare, some of whom are also in the child welfare system, to secure employment.

The Overlap: Parents in the Child Welfare System with AOD Problems

With an estimated 13 million children living with a parent who reportedly has used illicit drugs in the past year and some 28.6 million children living in alcoholic households [Colliver et al. 1994], a significant number of children may be at risk of maltreatment. But not all of these children will become victims of child abuse or neglect and, obviously, not all of those who are victims will be reported to public agencies.

Table 1. Paths of Exposure to Alcohol and Other Drug Use

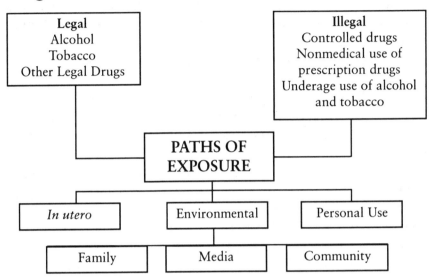

Though researchers have yet to accurately document the prevalence of substance abuse problems among families within the child welfare system, most have come to agree that 40 to 80% of parents with children in the child welfare system have AOD-related problems serious enough to affect their parenting. Below are just a few of the studies documenting the overlap:

- Of the nearly 1 million children found to be substantiated victims of child abuse and neglect in 1995, at least 50% had chemically involved caregivers [CWLA 1997].

- For two consecutive years, more than three-fourths of states (76% in 1996 and 80% in 1995) reported that substance abuse is one of the top two conditions assessed as problems for families reported for maltreatment [Wang & Daro 1997].

- Famularo and his colleagues found that more than two-thirds (67%) of child maltreatment cases involved a substance-abusing parent [Jaudes et al. 1995].

In addition, studies indicate that parental substance abuse is associated with *recurrent* reports of child abuse and neglect. Wolock and Magura concluded that parental substance abuse of any kind results in an increased likelihood of a subsequent report to CPS, and the effect of drugs and alcohol combined is particularly strong. Here are some additional findings:

- Children who are prenatally exposed to drugs are two to three times more likely to be abused than other children. In their study of more than 500 infants exposed prenatally to illicit substances, reports of abuse were subsequently filed for close to one-third (30%) of the children, two-thirds of which were substantiated. Of the substantiated cases, 51% were abused once, 37% twice, and 12% three or more times [Jaudes et al. 1995].

- A study of families reported to CPS who were followed for an average of two years found that in 55% of the families, one or both caretakers were identified as having a substance abuse problem. One or more recurrent reports were reported in just over half of these families [Wolock & Magura 1996].

"In the Best Interests of the Child"

A couple attending training for prospective foster parents were impressed when the trainer wrote "best interests of the child" on the board early in the session, thinking that the literature on parent-child interactions would be discussed. However, throughout their four training sessions, there was no further discussion of what the phrase meant in practice.

What *does* "best interests of the child" mean in AOD cases? There seem to be three levels of answers to the question:

- What the child needs in terms of immediate safety: who is competent right now to serve as caretaker on a daily basis?

- What the child needs him/herself: what level of intervention or treatment will best strengthen the protective factors needed to break the cycle of AOD abuse for that child?

- What the child needs in the longer term: what is the best possible relationship with his/her birth parents that will lead to family stability in later life?

The Effect of Substance Abuse on the Foster Care System

As Cole and her colleagues point out: "Whatever the prevalence of children exposed to drugs and alcohol in the general population, there can be little doubt that the vast majority of children entering foster care are affected by living in substance-abusing families" [Cole et al. 1996]. And the number of children entering foster care continues to skyrocket—in 1996, the figure topped 500,000, a 47% increase from the 340,000 cases in 1988 [DHHS 1997].

It is estimated that substance abuse is a factor in three-fourths of all placements. Children under 5 are the most vulnerable to abuse or neglect by a substance-abusing parent and represent the fastest growing population in out-of-home care [Day et al. 1998]. Several studies highlight the prevalence of AOD-problems among foster care cases:

- The U.S. General Accounting Office recently found that parental substance abuse was a factor for 78% of the children entering foster care in Los Angeles, New York City, and Philadelphia County [GAO 1994].

- In a recent CWLA survey, state child welfare agencies estimated that parental chemical dependency was a contributing factor in the out-of-home placement of at least 53% of the child protection cases [CWLA 1997].

- In that same survey, more than two-thirds (67%) of state child welfare agencies said that AOD-involved families are "much more likely" or "more likely" to reenter the child welfare system over a five-year period, compared to non-AOD-involved families [CWLA 1997].

- In Washington state, 41% of infants placed in out-of-home care in 1995 were born to mothers who abused alcohol or other drugs during their pregnancy.

Effects of Alcohol and Other Drug Abuse on a Parent's Ability to Care for Children

Use of alcohol and other drugs can seriously compromise a parent's capacity to protect a child, and such use interferes with the individual's general functioning in a number of ways. Bays [1990] stated that up to 90% of drug abusers have mental, emotional, or personality disorders that can compromise their ability to care for their children and influence poor parenting skills. More specifically, AOD use, abuse, and dependence can have the following effects [Besharov 1992]:

- Interfere with thought processes and thus consistent parenting processes—a parent's mental functioning, judgment, inhibitions, and protective capacity may become impaired.

- Interfere with the ability to respond consistently and sensitively to a child—a parent may be less sensitive, responsible, and accessible to infants. This can decrease the development of secure attachments between mother and child.

- Leave the parent emotionally and physically unavailable to a child—caseworkers may have difficulty getting a parent to focus on needs of the child.

- Lower a parent's threshold of aggression toward children.

- Result in a parent spending household money needed for food, clothing, and other basic needs on alcohol and other drugs.

- Be associated with criminal activity that may jeopardize a child's health and safety.

- Lead to the neglect of a child's routine health care needs, including well-baby checkups and immunization schedules.

Changing Practice and Policy

In recognition of the growing scope of this problem, policy reflected in recent federal and state legislation and in innovative practice in several communities shows a new emphasis on working with AOD services and agencies to help achieve the goals of the child welfare system. Efforts to strengthen the connections between these agencies have taken several forms:

- Set-asides from each system to work with children and families served by both systems,

- Federal waivers in one state (Delaware) to work with AOD-affected families in CWS* caseloads,

- State efforts to develop new and blended AOD-CWS risk assessments,

- State action to include AOD treatment in supportive services for welfare clients under Temporary Assistance for Needy Families (TANF),

- Proposals (in federal legislation not yet passed) to expand the use of CWS funding for treatment services, and

---

* Throughout this document, we refer to CWS (child welfare services). This is intended to mean the full range of child welfare agencies that address issues of out-of-home care, including foster care, adoption, and other forms of permanency planning. Child protective services (CPS) are mandated to address child safety issues, while CWS agencies have larger concerns with child well-being and family functioning. When we are discussing the narrower concern within CPS units for risk assessment and the actions taken by CPS units to ensure child safety, we will shift the focus of the guidebook from the larger CWS arena to the CPS units within it.

What's the Payoff?

The stakes in building bridges between CWS and AOD systems are significant: using the mid-point estimate of 60% of parents in the child welfare system affected by AOD problems, it is clear that a substantial net savings results from AOD treatment, even if it is assumed that treatment is effective for *only a portion of these parents* (detailed numbers are set forth in Chapter 4).

- An in-depth, federal study of how child welfare and AOD treatment services can connect more effectively (required by the Adoption and Safe Families Act of 1997).

Efforts by several prominent organizations, including the Child Welfare League of America (CWLA), have spotlighted these issues in the past few years.* CWLA's Chemical Dependency and Child Welfare Task Force, first convened in 1990, was reestablished in 1997 and continues its work at present. With funding from the U.S. Office of Juvenile Justice and Delinquency Prevention and as part of Secretary Shalala's National Initiative on Youth Substance Abuse Prevention, the CWLA task force is developing several projects to strengthen services for children and families experiencing AOD problems in child welfare. (This guidebook is one of those projects.)

At the same time, in several innovative sites around the nation, child welfare practice has been changing through new training curricula, out-stationing staff in such other settings as schools and family resource centers, links with juvenile justice agencies and the courts, community partnerships that bring AOD and CWS staff together with

---

* Some of these organizations include the Children's Defense Fund, the American Humane Association, Drug Strategies, the American Public Welfare Association, the National Association of State Drug and Alcohol Directors, Legal Action Center, and the Center for Substance Abuse Treatment in the U.S. Department of Health and Human Services. Funding for AOD-CWS demonstration projects has come from the Edna McConnell Clark Foundation, the Robert Wood Johnson Foundation, the Annie E. Casey Foundation, the Stuart Foundation, and others.

neighborhood residents in decentralized service models, and negotiated agreements for referral to and assessment by treatment agencies.

In recent years, the concern for the children affected by substance abuse has broadened well beyond the most visible examples of the need for connection between CWS and AOD: infants born with evidence of prenatal drug exposure. While tragic, these children represent fewer than 5% of all the children significantly affected by their parents' substance abuse [Young 1997]. Many of the innovations described in this guidebook began with a focus on prenatal drug exposure but moved to embrace the full range of problems among children and youth affected by alcohol and other drugs.

There has also been a growing recognition of the cumulative effects on children of the combination of AOD abuse and child abuse or neglect [Levoy et al. 1990]. The juvenile justice system has devoted particular attention to the relationships between child abuse and delinquency, focusing in several recent studies on the correlations between earlier child abuse and later delinquent behavior. Some studies have concluded that parents' AOD problems are especially powerful risk factors for youth, making it more likely that they will have problems in adolescence and later life [Rivinus 1991]. Several demonstration projects are targeting children who are most likely to "age into" the juvenile justice system from their earlier exposure to the CWS system, or those who have already become known to both systems.

C A S E **The Sacramento County Case Study.** In 1993,
S T U D Y Sacramento County's Department of Health and Human Services (DHHS) responded to the growing number of child protective cases in the County that involved AOD-related problems. With an estimated 2,000 drug-exposed infants born annually and requests for AOD services accounting for nearly 30% of all Family Preservation service requests, the DHHS leadership assessed the agency's capacity to meet these needs and concluded that at best it could respond to no more than 25% of the need. The Department, under the leadership of then-Director Robert Caulk, developed a multifaceted initiative focused on changing the child welfare and other systems through training and making AOD assessment and intervention part of the respon-

sibility of every worker. The clear and ambitious goal: to provide "direct AOD treatment on demand." The Department developed three levels of training for more than 2,000 employees, providing core information on chemical dependence in the first level, teaching advanced assessment and intervention skills in the second level, and building group treatment skills in the third level.

A rich set of lessons is emerging from several years of demonstration projects supported by private foundations as well as by state and federal governments. These include the Community Partnerships of the Clark Foundation, the Family to Family Projects of the Casey Foundation, demonstration projects sponsored and funded by the National Committee on Child Abuse and Neglect, studies funded by the U.S. Office of Juvenile Justice and Delinquency Prevention, and the "Starting Early/Starting Smart" project, a joint effort of the Casey Family Program and the Substance Abuse and Mental Health Administration, which includes grants for programs addressing the needs of children age 0-7 who are at high risk of developing problems related to the AOD or mental health problems of their parents.

This guidebook draws on the lessons from several of these demonstration projects. In many ways, however, some of the most instructive lessons emerge from a single case study: Sacramento County's four-year (and ongoing) initiative, which has addressed CWS-AOD issues in a larger context of other systems, including welfare, criminal justice, and health services. Thus, the Sacramento case study of CWS-AOD connections is featured throughout this guidebook, illustrating many lessons for other projects and other communities.

Interaction with Other Systems: TANF, Juvenile Justice, Family Violence, and Mental Health

Some of the urgency in recent bridge-building efforts stems from the potential impact on child welfare agencies of the 1996 federal legislation that created the Temporary Assistance for Needy Families (TANF) program. While we lack comprehensive data as to how many clients are enrolled concurrently in TANF, child protective services caseloads, and AOD treatment, numerous studies have documented that these multiproblem families are the highest risk clients in each of these systems [Young & Gardner 1997].

Although this guidebook will focus primarily on CWS-AOD linkage, it will also examine the emerging models of TANF-AOD connections, since welfare reform changes are certain to affect child welfare caseloads in years to come. Substantial CWS impacts are predicted both by the welfare reform optimists (who believe that children will be much better off in families with parents working and free of welfare dependence), and by the pessimists (who believe that neglect cases will increase substantially as parents who are removed from welfare find they cannot hold jobs). Which of these proves true, and for which children and families, will depend upon implementation decisions made in communities throughout the nation. Understanding the impacts of welfare reform will also require that communities make serious efforts to monitor the effects of reform beyond simple measures such as caseload reduction.

Three other systems need to be considered in the process of enhancing the connections between CWS and AOD services: (1) the related areas of juvenile justice, delinquency prevention, and youth development; (2) family violence; and (3) mental health. In addition to TANF, these are the parallel systems, combined with the indispensable roles of parents and the wider community, that have the resources to promote family stability. If these separate systems cannot forge closer links, each will be forced to work within its own limited resources, when it is clear that the resources of more than one system are needed to address the needs of families with multiple problems. The practices and policies of other systems play crucial roles in the future of the child welfare system, leading to a powerful paradox: the well-being of many children and the future of child welfare is heavily dependent on decisions made *outside* the child welfare system, in the form of both daily practice and public policy.

The Need for a Policy Framework

In recent work in this area, a six-part framework has proven a useful way to organize discussion of the policy issues raised when CWS and AOD agencies and programs are brought together.* The policy framework includes values, daily practice, training, outcomes and information systems, budgets, and service delivery. The elements serve as a template for developing and assessing initiatives that go beyond pilot projects to attempt system-level change. It should not be applied as a simple checklist, however. These six elements are interdependent, as revealed in the Sacramento initiative described below and in several other model projects. Although it is obviously possible to launch projects that feature innovations in only one or two of these dimensions, the most important premise of the framework is that working *solely* within a single area will ultimately fail, because the other ingredients are missing or not addressed in depth. Innovation has to begin somewhere, and carefully choosing the correct entry point in each policy setting is the first step, which must be followed by working across all six areas.

These elements also help us understand why it is difficult to link CWS and AOD services, despite the excellent efforts undertaken by those agencies and communities (described on page 27 and following). In each of these areas, there are formidable barriers to connecting the two systems—and to working with other systems as well.

The Importance of Bridging the Practice-Policy Gap

The policy framework proposed in this guidebook is based on a conviction that the worlds of policy and practice remain too far apart in both CWS and AOD arenas. Attempts to change daily practice *necessarily* require policy change, or they become isolated pilot projects that cannot be sustained or expanded. Practice can raise important

---

* This framework draws upon a 1997 report that the authors prepared for the Stuart Foundation, *Bridge Building: An Action Plan for State and County Efforts to Strengthen Links between Child Welfare Services and Services for Alcohol and Other Drug Problems.* Irvine, CA: Children and Family Futures.

questions about the lack of CWS-AOD connections, but it requires a policy process to respond to these problems with more than *ad hoc*, crisis-driven, temporary fixes. At the same time, without changes in practice, the policy process often operates to ratify and protect the status quo, which is always the least disruptive policy to implement.

So, practice and policy must be considered together when attempting to effect meaningful change. But the usual relationship between the two worlds ranges from benign ignorance to outright disdain. Those more familiar with the policy world may perceive hands-on practitioners as too overwhelmed by their work to see "the big picture" of resources and legislation, while practitioners may regard those from the policy sector as hopelessly unrealistic, far removed from the realities of daily practice and the dynamics of working with challenging clients in troubled communities.

A closer, mutually respectful relationship is needed between the world of the "hands-on" line staff and the world of the policymakers and budget staffs. Bringing together these two worlds is essential to build the bridges between CWS and AOD, since many policy issues that cut across the two sectors need action in both policy and practice realms:

- The impact of state and local budget decisions about CWS staffing and caseloads;

- The need to develop a resource strategy that breaks out of the pilot project mentality to create and carry out a design for going to full scale—redirecting significant core agency budgets and neighborhood assets, rather than relying solely on external grants;

- The concentration of resources on specific neighborhoods in ways that may affect overall citywide or countywide allocations;

- The impact of assessment practice in changing policy to direct resources to clients who need help; and

- The potential for securing new resources from other agencies that can support community partnerships with AOD services, family violence services, child care, and school-linked services.

These are all policy issues, in the sense that policy consists of choosing a course of action and putting resources behind it. But these choices can and must be informed and shaped by the realities of daily practice undertaken by skilled professionals, helpers, and parents. Practice needs to inform policy; policy needs to provide a framework for rational decisions that support the best kinds of practice. Policy can institutionalize best practices, ensure that they can be sustained, and provide the resources to assess their effectiveness in helping clients and communities. Practice changes are unlikely to survive unless policy supporting those changes is put in place prior to their expansion.

Why Values Matter

It is impossible to think and work effectively on issues of child abuse, substance abuse, and poverty without understanding how deep-seated our underlying values are on these issues. Our attitudes about how to treat children are learned and taught in our cultures from the earliest days of family life. Our attitudes toward legal and illegal drugs are the product of centuries of public opinion in this nation, going back to Prohibition, the Puritan era, and beyond. And the ways we think about the causes of poverty are at least four centuries old, dating from the Elizabethan Poor Laws and coming down to the intense debates over welfare reform in the mid-1990s. Sometimes we stereotype when we think and talk about these difficult issues.* When we do, it becomes more difficult to make policy or change practice, because the ingrained ways of thinking about these issues in polarized language force the middle ground options out of the debate.

---

* Children and Family Futures believes that the values framework in which we discuss these issues is so important that it must be addressed as a critical part of any community's efforts to work collaboratively. We have developed a Collaborative Values Inventory as a neutral tool used to reveal the underlying values that collaborations often submerge in their desire to avoid conflict. This tool is attached as Appendix A.

As we noted in the Winter 1998 issue of *Public Welfare* [Young & Gardner 1998], some individuals and some workers believe that society should take children away from their parents if the parents are abusing drugs. The subject becomes more difficult, however, when we recognize that millions of children live in middle-income homes where substance use—and substance abuse—are common occurrences that do not come to the attention of protective services agencies. The distinctions among *use, abuse,* and *chemical dependence* are crucial to understanding the interplay among dependence, neglect, child abuse, poverty, and a lack of job skills. Our ability to decide accurately when AOD abuse and dependence endanger children has not grown as fast as our recognition that millions of children are undeniably affected by their parents' AOD problems.

We believe that there is a middle ground in which both sets of underlying values—child safety and family stability—can be endorsed while designing systems that achieve a balanced set of obligations:

- Placing the responsibility on parents to do everything they can to provide a safe and supportive home for their children, and

- Placing the responsibility on society and its service systems to provide parents with the resources they need to end their chemical dependence and its harmful effects on their children.

Children's needs will not be met by either a strict demand for abstinence or, at the other extreme, the too-frequent practice of ignoring substance abuse problems until they become severe enough to move toward terminating parents' custody rights. Yet the public debate over these issues tends to swing from pole to pole, rarely confronting the hard choices necessary to ensure that parents are given a fair chance to recover and that children are given a fair chance to live in nurturing homes with loving caretakers.

The recent legislative history of AOD issues in social welfare and child welfare is instructive, revealing the preoccupation of some lawmakers with sanctioning clients who abuse drugs and punishing those with past drug felonies. In the TANF legislation, references to drug testing and prohibitions aimed at clients convicted of drug felonies were the only AOD issues addressed in the law. But the federal law was silent on what to do about the estimated 1 million women who may need treatment to enable them to perform effectively at new jobs. In some states, however, more in-depth approaches to the issue included set-asides of specific resources for treatment of TANF clients.

The Adoption and Safe Families Act of 1997 signed by the President last November originally included detailed provisions and funding for building closer ties between child welfare and AOD agencies. But unable to agree on how to respond to overlapping substance abuse and child abuse issues, Congress removed all provisions to providing AOD treatment with child welfare funding and charged DHHS with conducting a study of the issue.

The Policy Framework in Action

The Element	The Impact and Trends
Daily practice	Assessment, caseloads, and incentives
Training	Working across agency boundaries with new AOD content
Outcomes and information systems	The shift toward client outcomes and results-based accountability
Budgets	Shifting from categorical funding to blended and linked funding
Service delivery	Alternative delivery methods, including for-profits, faith-based organizations, community-based partnerships, and managed care organizations.

Daily Practice

Ensuring the competence and thoroughness of daily practices of line CWS and AOD workers is critical to making lasting change. Some training initiatives have encountered problems because they did not recognize that without new incentive systems, newly trained workers would have little reason to use new practices in their day-to-day work with clients. The fundamental connection between client and worker is at the heart of AOD diagnosis and treatment, and different approaches to that all-important relationship are described below. *Assessment*, the process at the core of how workers make judgments about their clients, is discussed in Chapter 5, since it constitutes and influences much of daily practice in both the CWS and AOD systems.

Training

Training is a crucial element in system innovations, but training alone cannot achieve system reform. Furthermore, most training today is categorical, operating as though the system in which it operates were the only system in which workers function. We frequently hear complaints by workers and supervisors in both CWS and AOD systems who state that they know far too little about the other systems with which they should be working more closely. (After the new training of more than 1,000 Sacramento County health and human services staff and others from community agencies and other county departments, workers strongly expressed their positive responses, as quoted later in this report.)

Outcomes and Information Systems

For good practice to lead to better outcomes, it must be accompanied by a move toward results-based accountability. The use of defined outcomes as client-level measures of a program's impact, rather than measuring the units of services provided or the number of clients served, has accelerated in the past decade as a critical management trend affecting both child welfare and the treatment field. Under pressure from managed care in general and behavioral health firms specifically, outcomes-based evaluation has progressed further in the AOD field than in the CWS arena. But to date, funding organizations (both government agencies and private foundations) have not fully adopted results-based evaluation or results-specific budgeting for either CWS or AOD agencies [Gardner 1996]. Agencies are collecting and using outcomes, but budget decisions are not linked to outcomes in any sustained way in most child welfare or AOD treatment agencies. Some of the most basic information about what happens to clients is not collected by child welfare agencies or by many treatment agencies.

C A S E Comprehensive Training. Sacramento implemented its training based on the fundamental
S T U D Y belief that "department members from every
level...must have the capacity to address alcohol
and other drug issues." This basic premise should underlie
all such efforts. The prerequisite to a serious commitment to
training is a recognition that the great majority of workers in
the child welfare system and in the treatment agencies do not
know enough about "the other side" to work effectively across
systems.

As CWLA summed up in 1997: "...a majority of state child welfare agencies are not equipped to deal with chemically involved clients. Many agencies do not have data collection processes, assessment protocols, policies, or programs that are responsive to youths'
AOD needs" [CWLA 1997].

Budgets

Connecting CWS and AOD agencies must happen in a world of
categorical funding. Despite growing familiarity with "wraparound
funding," new legislation that enables blended funding, and the success of some well-funded demonstration programs in tapping dozens
of sources from different state and federal agencies and private foundations, the world of daily practice remains a world of categorical
policy making and categorical funding streams. That context eventually constrains all efforts to link programs funded from different sources
and makes it far more difficult to assemble resources, train workers, and
refer and treat clients across the boundaries of these separate systems.

Service Delivery

The final element of the policy framework is *how* services are
actually delivered, whether through the efforts of CWS workers, nonprofit contractors, behavioral health firms operating managed care
contracts, faith-based organizations, or neighborhood-based family
support organizations. The shift to expanded use of both managed
care and community-based networks of agencies needs to be taken
into account in describing recent changes in the ways these services
are delivered.

Don't Ask, Don't Tell

For all the progress made in recent years in both CWS and AOD agencies, it is important to recognize that the norm in many sites is still a gap between the two. To quote one California county administrator from a child welfare agency, "For years the workers have been saying [AOD] isn't on the form and it usually isn't in the allegation, so I don't go looking for it." In the same conversation, an AOD agency official admitted, "We have just not seen children as part of our responsibility."

Barriers to CWS-AOD Links

The barriers to CWS-AOD connections loom large in each area of the policy framework. Potential conflicts in values and philosophies held by each domain occur over such fundamental issues as, "Who really is the client, the parent or the child?" There are many other differences between the CWS and AOD systems that make it difficult to develop links, including differences in the style of daily practice by line staff, how they screen and assess clients' needs, the education and background of workers, how each system measures and defines success for its clients, what data it collects about its clients, the funding streams and the financial assumptions of the two systems, and ways in which the two systems are moving toward both managed care and neighborhood-based service delivery.

One AOD practitioner summarized the barriers between the two systems in strong language:

> I don't believe the substance abuse system has wanted to embrace responsibility for assisting in the determination of child placement and operationalizing the role of addiction and recovery in child protection ... I also think that most child protection workers don't believe that treatment works, and when added to the issues around difficult access, relapse, sequential case planning, treatment is just another variable to deal with in disposition of the case ... This results in con-

secutive and incompatible case management rather than con-current planning . . . As the substance abuse field has been able to assist the criminal justice system in making determi-nations between incarceration and treatment, so we must become more adept in assisting the child welfare system in the determinations for which they are responsible, when sub-stance abuse is a factor [personal communication 1998].

All of these pose major challenges to the effort needed to bridge the gap between the two systems. Considering the many obstacles to coordination of CWS-AOD agencies, the achievements of states, com-munities, and agencies that we describe in Chapter 2 are all the more impressive; the models show how innovative practices and policies can work together to overcome barriers.*

Timing Barriers: The "Four Clocks"

A key barrier that needs specific attention is what we term the "four clocks problem"—the four completely different timetables that can affect children and parents in an AOD-abusing family:

- The child welfare system timetable of six-month reviews of a parent's progress, which the new federal legislation accelerates to a requirement for a permanency hearing at 12 months.

- The timetable for treatment and recovery, which often takes much longer than AOD-based funding allows, and which is often incompatible with child welfare deadlines for par-ents who may have relapsed but are still working at their recovery; some have summarized the AOD timetable as "one day at a time, for the rest of your life."

---

* A full discussion of the barriers between the systems can be found in sev-eral previous works, including the following: Child Welfare League of America (1992). *Children at the front.* Washington, DC: Author; Gardner, S. L., & Young, N. K. (1997). *Bridge building*; and Gardner, S. L., & Young, N. K. (1996). *The implications of alcohol and other drug-related problems for community-wide family support systems.* Cambridge, MA: The John F. Kennedy School of Government, Harvard University.

- The timetable now imposed for TANF (former AFDC) clients who must find work in 24 months. (This is the federal maximum; some states have lower limits and thus some clients are already reaching the cutoff point.)

- The developmental timetable that affects children, especially younger children, as they achieve bonding and attachment—or fail to—as they pass through the period of the first 18 months, which new research on brain development has shown to be a critical period of time in a young child's life.

Barriers in Defining the Client

A further basis for the problems between the two systems arises in the competing demands for AOD services for populations other than children and families. In part due to the improving information base about what kinds of treatment are most effective for which kinds of clients, demands for AOD support services have multiplied from the criminal justice system, the mental health system, and now, notably, the overlapping welfare/TANF system. Treatment for inmates has been an area of increasing emphasis, given the number of drug offenders in state prisons and local jails. Resources in the AOD system are scarce in the short run, and the call for expanded responsiveness to the special needs of children and families in the CPS system conflicts in important ways with these other demands. With waiting lists for different kinds of clients, those with special claims in the eyes of their sponsoring agencies may not meet the same priorities in other agencies.

For a CPS worker, the client is both the child and the family, with the risk to the child as the primary short-term concern and the safety of the child the longer range priority. But for a worker in the AOD treatment system, clients are addicts and alcoholics, usually adults, and their status as a parent is generally irrelevant unless they are in one of the few perinatal programs or a special program for mothers and their children. In most treatment programs, the children of clients may not be seen as important; they may be cited as an incentive for recovery, but are usually not involved in any active way themselves. The AOD worker also may identify with the client because she/he is likely to be recovering from addiction and more readily understands the client's problems and the mechanisms of denial and avoidance.

In contrast, a CPS worker dealing with a known substance abuser is generally frustrated and sometimes even angry at such a parent, because of the risks to the child. Depending upon the worker's own attitudes, the client may be seen as suffering from a powerful disease for which treatment must be sought—but is more typically viewed as a selfish, thoughtless parent with no regard for her or his child. Judges and the court system can accentuate these attitudes when they adopt a "zero-tolerance" approach that emphasizes solely punitive measures and reflects little understanding of AOD treatment or parental functioning.

The differences between the CPS and AOD systems' responses to licit and illicit drugs are also important barriers at times. Practitioners have pointed out how CPS focuses on illegal substances and overlooks alcohol abuse and its consequences on the family, despite the much greater overall damage done to children both prenatally and environmentally by alcohol.

Differences in agency perspectives on who is the client also lead to issues of confidentiality, which are discussed at greater length in Chapter 6.

Barriers of Different Training and Education

Workers in the two systems are trained differently and tend to have different educational backgrounds. The content of training in the two systems rarely addresses the connections between the systems or methods that could be used to work across systems in identifying and assessing AOD-related problems.

A recent review of CWS training in universities documented the lack of emphasis upon addiction issues as they affect children and the complexities of working across the two systems. Most of what is included focuses on perinatal substance abuse and the issues of the positive toxicology screen at birth. These "doses" of exposure to AOD issues appear disproportionately small, compared to the importance of these issues in CWS work. As one trainer put it, while working in a program that provides an in-service orientation to addiction for health and human services professionals who work across CPS-AOD agency lines, "What we are doing here is remedial—they should have gotten all this in their preservice programs."

Workers in the AOD system are trained in a wide variety of fields. A significant percentage of them have come through the treatment system themselves. While some have advanced degrees in counseling and other fields, many frontline workers have little formal training. This is especially true when mutual aid programs are factored into the spectrum of AOD treatment programs. In these self-help oriented systems, the "helpers" are lay people who draw heavily on their own experience rather than on formal education.

Funding Barriers

The funding barriers that impair CWS-AOD connections include the complexity of categorical funding, the barriers to reimbursement for many of the treatment needs of parents and adolescents, and a tendency of each "side" of the CWS-AOD relationship to protect its own funding sources and seek allocations from the other. Representatives of the two groups would doubtless add a fundamental resources gap in total spending to the list of funding barriers. Waiting lists in some states and communities provide evidence of this barrier, despite the absence in most communities of any total inventory of AOD spending. Federal earmarks are cited by some AOD providers as funding barriers to working with CWS clients, although the national allocation of approximately 27% of all publicly funded treatment slots to women reflects state priorities for providing treatment to men, especially those in prison, rather than federal requirements for such a division of funding.

The funding barriers also lead to problems caused by the inability of either CWS or AOD agencies to control their own resources, due to two major external forces: the decisions of courts and the decisions of managed care firms in the behavioral health field. In both cases, resource decisions are significantly out of the hands of the CWS or AOD agencies, which means that when the two sets of agencies do seek to cooperate, outside mandates may make it more difficult because of a requirement set by a court or a regulatory burden of proof created by a managed care firm that makes it difficult to arrange appropriate treatment for some clients. Without education and training aimed at these key external decision makers who affect CWS-AOD links, barriers from outside the two sets of agencies will continue to affect bridge-building efforts launched from within these agencies.

Is a Policy Framework Realistic?

It can be argued that policy making on issues as difficult as child abuse, substance abuse, and family violence is *unavoidably* crisis-driven, episodic, and incremental at best. In such an environment, innovation is difficult to launch and even more difficult to sustain beyond the level of pilot projects. But there are a sufficient number of states and communities that have developed such sustained innovation in recent years, under the pressures of rising caseloads and greater understanding about the problems of substance abuse, to justify the attempt to set forth and refine a framework that could better guide policy making in a more comprehensive, less fragmented fashion.

The quest is not for rigidly coordinated, fully rationalized policy; it is rather for policy that goes beyond reacting to symptoms and crises to address the underlying forces that affect child abuse. Such policy can emerge from a framework, as described in this guidebook, that views inevitable crisis as an opportunity for reform, rather than a demand for quick fixes with more regard for media spin than the lives of children.

References

Anderson, M., Elk, R., and Andres, R. (1997). Social, ethical, and practical aspects of perinatal substance use. *Journal of Substance Abuse Treatment, 14* (5), 481-86.

Bays, J. (1990). Substance abuse and child abuse impact on addiction on the child. *Pediatric Clinics of North America, 37* (4), 881-905.

Besharov, D. (1992). *When drug addicts have children.* Washington, DC: American Enterprise Institute and Child Welfare League of America

Child Welfare League of America. (1997). *Alcohol and other drug survey of state child welfare agencies.* Draft report, unpublished. Washington, DC: Author.

Cole, E., Barth, R., Crocker, A., & Moss, K. (1996). *Policy and practice challenges in serving infants and young children whose parents abuse drugs and alcohol,* Boston, MA: Family Builders Network.

Day, P., Robison, S., & Sheikh, L. (1998). *Ours to keep: Building a community assessment strategy for child protection.* Washington, DC: Child Welfare League of America; see also National Center on Addiction and Substance Abuse at Columbia University, http://www.casacolumbia.org.

Gardner, S. L. (1996). *Moving toward outcomes: An overview of the state of the art and key lessons for agencies.* Honolulu, HI: The Hawaii Community Services Council.

Gregoire, T. (1994). Assessing the benefits and increasing the utility of addiction training for public child welfare workers: A pilot study. *Child Welfare, 73*(1), 69-81.

Jaudes, P., Ekwo, E., & Voorhis, J. (1995). Association of drug abuse and child abuse. *Child Abuse and Neglect, 19*(9), 1065-1075.

Levoy, D., Rivinus, T.M., Matzko, M., & McGuire, J. (1990). *Children in search of a diagnosis: Chronic trauma disorder of childhood.* New York: Brunner/Mazel Publishers.

Reid, G., Sigurdson, E., Wright, A., & Christianson-Wood, J. (1996). Risk assessment: Some Canadian findings. *Protecting Children, 12,* 24-31.

Rivinus, T.M. (Ed.) (1991). *Children of chemically dependent parents: Multiperspectives from the cutting edge.* New York: Brunner/Mazel Publishers.

U.S. Department of Health and Human Services. (September 17, 1997). *HHS invests in America's children*. Fact Sheet available online at http://www.os.dhhs.gov.

U.S. General Accounting Office. (1994). *Foster care: Parental drug abuse has alarming impact on young children*. Washington, DC: Author.

Wolock, I., & Magura, S. (1996). Parental substance abuse as a predictor of child maltreatment re-reports. *Child Abuse and Neglect*, 20(12), 1183-93.

Young, N. K. (1997). Effects of alcohol and other drugs on children. *Journal of Psychoactive Drugs*, 19(1), 23-42. The 5% estimate is based on the percentage of all prenatally exposed cases that were referred to the county CPS agency in Los Angeles County in 1993, compared with estimates of the wide incidence of effects on children affected by drugs and alcohol by family and environmental sources, using national figures drawn from a variety of sources.

Young, N. K., & Gardner, S. L. (1997). *Implementing welfare reform: Solutions to the substance abuse problem*, Washington, DC: Drug Strategies and Irvine, CA: Children and Family Futures.

Young, N. K. & Gardner, S. L. (1998). Children at the crossroads. *Public Welfare*, 56(1), 3-10.

2

Seeking Solutions

Models of Current CWS-AOD Links

To understand how child welfare agencies are responding to AOD problems, we need to examine the progress made in each of the five core areas of the policy framework. The successes and impressive pilot projects described in this section represent a substantial body of work in the decade or more since the interrelatedness of CWS and AOD problems first attracted national attention. We have sought to distill the essential knowledge from hundreds of practitioners, policymakers, and advocates; their voices can be heard throughout this guidebook.

Based on the policy framework that we have described and on nine model strategies, the matrix shown in Table 2 (on page 28) summarizes the state of the art in efforts to address AOD problems among child welfare cases [Young & Gardner 1998]. Some sites that have employed a particular model have been operational for three or four years, while others are in the early demonstration stages. But the range of options shows how different states and communities have approached the tasks of building new links across systems and with communities.

The noted sites are examples of programs based on these models; these are not the only sites where these approaches are being pursued. Some of the innovative projects and initiatives described in this chapter focus on only one of the features included in the matrix, while others have been designed as comprehensive initiatives and incorporate more than one facet of the framework.

Following our discussion of these model approaches that work across CWS and AOD systems, we turn to several innovative practices *within* the child welfare field and examine how these innovations interact with the growing effort to respond to AOD problems. Because of the great importance we attach to *assessment practice* as

Table 2. Model Strategies and the Policy Framework

Model Strategies	Elements of the Policy Framework				
	Daily Practice	Training	Outcomes & Info. Systems	Budgets	Service Delivery
Paired AOD Counselor & CWS Worker (DE)	Joint family visits and case planning	Formal cross-training	Separate assessment and MIS, evaluation in place	Title IV-E waiver	Joint case planning and management
AOD Counselor Out-stationed at a CWS Office as Technical Assistance (NJ)	AOD worker as resource in CWS office	Informal and formal cross-training	Separate assessment and MIS	Joint-funded AOD/CWS	Provides immediate access to AOD assistance to CWS
AOD Screener in CWS/Welfare Office; CWS & Welfare Staff on Loan to State Office (OR)	CWS worker makes referral to screener who refers to treatment	Informal and formal cross-training	Separate assessment and MIS	Joint-funded AOD/CWS/welfare	Establishes gatekeeper to AOD treatment resources
Multidisciplinary Team for Joint Case Planning (women's treatment programs, multiple sites)	Parallel workers with families who meet for joint planning	Informal cross-training	Separate multiple assessments	Separate funds from each partner agency	Joint case conferencing opportunities, sometimes "overall case manager"
Paired CWS Worker & Person in Recovery (Cleveland, OH)	CWS worker & PIR joint family visits, PIR provides support	Informal training of CWS	Joint assessment; only CWS MIS	Foundation grant and CWS funding	Increases the use of peer leaders as experts for CWS workers
Infusion of AOD Strategies through Training (Sacramento County)	CWS worker trainer to conduct "mini-interventions," assess for treatment, make referral & expand AOD capacity	In-depth formalized training leading to treatment capacity expansion	AOD assessment for problem severity and initial match to level of care by trained CWS workers	Foundation grant and CWS funding	Attempts to create systemic change within CWS to recognize, intervene, & expand capacity for AOD problems
Community Partners of Recovery & Treatment Staff with CWS (Nashville, TN)	CWS worker can call for assistance from person in recovery or treatment staff	Informal cross-training	Separate assessment when families enter either system	Primarily AOD funding	Changes reporting requirements, foster family regulations
Community Partnerships for the Protection of Children (Jacksonville, Cedar Rapids, Louisville, St. Louis)	Community, CWS, and AOD joint problem solving	Cross-training and technical assistance	Self-evaluation protocols supported by technical assistance	Attempts to blend funding across systems	Governance through new community entity
Family Drug Court (Pensacola, Reno)	Frequent contact with judge with graduated sanctions	Judges seek own training	Separate assessment and MIS	Family court	Uses authority of court to increase compliance with AOD treatment

the process that bridges the CWS and AOD systems and that promotes interaction among and across all five of the framework elements, we also include a separate section that discusses innovation in screening and assessment of AOD problems as they affect referral of CWS parents to treatment.

Characteristics of the Models: Strengths and Concerns

Nine model strategies are included in the matrix. Salient features and issues of each model are summarized below:

Paired AOD Counselor and CWS Worker. The model relying on an AOD counselor paired with a CWS worker has the advantage of multiple staff resources, which is also its obvious disadvantage—its cost. The model also operates from an assumption which some practitioners question—that a specialist orientation is essential to working effectively with the family, rather than teaching each professional enough about the other set of functions to be able to make connections without dedicated specialized staff.

AOD Counselor Out-stationed at a CWS Office as Technical Assistance. The model based on AOD staff out-stationing brings the advantage of line staff expertise immediately available to work on a case, which may reduce the pressures felt by CWS workers or neighborhood workers dealing with substance abuse for the first time. However, AOD out-stationing by itself doesn't change the home institution from which the worker is out-stationed. Moreover, out-stationed workers can become isolated from the "home office," unable to command its resources beyond token levels.

AOD Screener in CWS/Welfare Office. When an AOD screener is added to the service unit, the screener functions as a gatekeeper for current AOD resources and may trigger more slots for CWS clients. CWS staff still function as intake screeners for referrals. AOD workers then screen clients, but they may refer on to an unchanged AOD system in which no new priority for CWS parents has been negotiated. In an interesting variation on this approach, Oregon has placed CWS and welfare staff on loan to the AOD office to deal with policy issues. This puts CWS and welfare expertise inside the AOD agency, rather than vice versa.

Multidisciplinary Team for Joint Case Planning. Multidisciplinary teams are perhaps the most thorough staff-level reform possible. But implementing this reform at more than pilot project levels demands a "theory of resources" (discussed in Chapter 3), since it is difficult to sustain such teams beyond the pilot project phase which may become a "Cadillac model" that is hard to support. Such pilot projects tend to drift into a system maintenance role because they are so costly, in contrast to promoting system change that permanently redirects staff resources toward institutionalizing such teams as a part of the normal staffing pattern.

Paired CWS Worker and Person in Recovery. Staffing a team with a recovering person provides strong rapport and access to clients, enabling the CWS worker to perform the sanctioning role while the recovering staff member can play a more supportive role. Relying on the unique expertise of a peer from the community can reduce the client's denial and avoidance problems, as the worker both empathizes with and challenges the client. The risk of this approach is role confusion and the difficulties of building an effective partnership with an uncredentialed lay person who may face the problems of adjusting to a system that does not value lay experience as much as professional credentials and time in service.

Infusion of AOD Strategies Through Training. The AOD infusion approach (used by Sacramento County and other sites) is, in our view, by far the most appropriate way to achieve genuine reform, working across the five core elements of the framework and going outside the CWS system to other systems, such as criminal justice and public health. But it is hard to sustain and is susceptible to external events and leadership changes. It is also difficult to get workers under normal or greater pressures to adopt new behaviors, especially new assessment tools, without careful advance planning and strong top- and mid-level leadership. Infusing the AOD perspective in a CWS agency requires a level of information systems and results-based accountability that many agencies are unlikely to have yet achieved. The infusion approach also expands the capacity of the AOD treatment system by moving away from treatment services narrowly defined as residential treatment, broadening the base of services to pretreatment and community support models. This approach can and should be combined with networks at the neighborhood level.

Community Partners of Recovery and Treatment Staff with CWS. The community partners approach draws community support in the form of active buy-in from local residents, but it is not clear that it seeks to change the system. In some sites, it has led to system changes to the extent that informal community support and interim caregiving have reduced the need for formal CWS filing, enabling the placement of children in safe environments while parents are enrolled in treatment.

Community Partnerships for the Protection of Children. The advantages of community partnerships include all the advantages of the prior approach, plus the advantage of a new governance entity that can address the need for a broad constituency base for systems change. However, decentralized pilot projects often reflect an initial preference by neighborhood groups for a gradual community-building effort that focuses primarily on "microprojects." Such projects may provide a foundation for larger, more strategic efforts, or they may lead to less emphasis on opportunities to affect the larger system's resources through a formal policy agenda. The effect of such partnerships in making these choices remains to be seen.

Family Drug Court. The Family Drug Court approach uses the impressive authority of the court, which is a substantial force for reform and can also mandate participation in treatment. However, reforms that are restricted to the court system may ignore the rest of the CWS-AOD systems and thus lack the resources to make court powers effective. Court systems have also found it difficult to divert scarce program funding to evaluations of the effectiveness of court-mandated programs to which their clients have been referred.

These summary comments on the nine models should make clear that these are evolving approaches. Some of the concerns we have expressed may not apply to all the sites that have adopted an approach, but we have sought to reflect what practitioners have said and what our own experience has shown about the advantages and drawbacks of these approaches. Described below are a few of the projects that are spotlighted in the matrix.

The Clark Community Partnerships

The Edna McConnell Clark Foundation's Community Partnership sites (Cedar Rapids, Iowa; St. Louis, Missouri; Louisville, Kentucky; and Jacksonville, Florida) are implementing a four-part strategy:

- Develop an individualized course of action for each child and family identified by community members as being at substantial risk of child abuse or neglect;

- Organize a network of neighborhood and community supports, including a neighborhood site for agency CWS staff, as well as neighborhood "helpers";

- Establish new policies and practices within the CWS agency, including consulting with partner agencies and intensifying focus on families with a recurrent pattern of child maltreatment; and

- Develop a collaborative decision-making capacity to sustain the partnership.

The strategy plan for the Clark projects explicitly emphasizes that both substance abuse and family violence have been included in the policy changes sought in the child welfare system:

> **Community Partnership Plan:** Sites are asked to ensure that as part of the development of each plan, assessment is made of whether substance abuse and domestic violence are problems for the family. If they are, the family's action plan is expected to include activities that will alleviate these problems. ... CWS agencies will establish close working relationships (and possible joint operating procedures) with domestic violence service providers and with substance abuse providers ... Substance abuse prevention and treatment programs must be immediately available within the network and to the CWS agency [Center for the Study of Social Policy 1997].

Each sites' assessment and action plan is to include a response to "reports of abuse and neglect with a *differential response* based on the severity of the situation and the future risk to the child." These efforts are expected to go beyond the formal agency networks to natural helpers and the staff of community-based agencies, such as child care providers, schools, faith-based organizations, and recreation agencies. CWS staff are being relocated into neighborhood locations, not only as a new work site, but to enable deeper family assessments and become familiar with and tap into local services and supports for families.

In Louisville, meetings have been held at the neighborhood level among providers and neighborhood residents, planning for "sober housing units" has begun in the target neighborhood, and a substance abuse coordinator has been hired for the project. In Jacksonville, community meetings have led to a set of proposals for neighborhood-level initiatives that are being prioritized for implementation in 1998. AOD treatment providers have joined CWS staff and neighborhood residents in an active planning group that has been addressing AOD issues.

The Delaware Title IV-E Waiver

Delaware is the only state that expressly targeted AOD problems in its application for a federal Title IV-E waiver. Granted in June 1996, Delaware's waiver was one of the initial 10 state waivers for child welfare agencies authorized by P.L. 103-432. (The Adoption and Safe Families Act legislation of 1997 authorizes DHHS to grant an additional 10 state waivers.) Under the waiver, the state is using foster care funds (Title IV-E) to fund substance abuse counselors and to co-locate them with child protective staff. A component of the evaluation is to ensure that the project is cost neutral to the federal government.

Listed below are the objectives of the project:

- Prevent or delay entry of children into out-of-home care because of parental substance abuse, or reduce the time in care in 50% of the families receiving multidisciplinary team services;

- Reduce the amount of time between identification of a substance abuse problem and completion of an evaluation and subsequent treatment; and

- Ensure permanency for children by verifying that reasonable efforts have been made to prevent placement and that appropriate reunification services have been made available.

The staff use a team approach, with the child protective worker focusing on child protection and safety issues and the substance abuse counselor identifying the extent of the AOD problem and its impact on child safety. The substance abuse counselor assists the family with linkages to treatment resources and provides support and treatment during the early stages of the AOD intervention. An extensive evaluation is being conducted using random assignment of cases to control and demonstration sites.*

The Starting Early/Starting Smart Program

The Casey Family Program, in conjunction with federal agencies (the Substance Abuse and Mental Health Services Administration [SAMHSA], the Health Resources and Services Administration [HRSA], the Administration on Children and Families [ACF], and the Department of Education) began an effort in 1997 to support five primary care and seven early childhood integrated service sites. One of these sites emphasizes child welfare populations: in Cook County, Illinois, foster parents for a group of children who have been removed from their families because of substance abuse will be provided extensive support while birth parents will be in treatment The demonstration's evaluation is conducted through a data coordination center that is studying two questions: (1) Will integrated services increase access to substance abuse and mental health services for children and families? (2) Will integrated services improve outcomes for the children and the families?**

---

* The contact person for Delaware's program is Candace R. Charkow, Treatment Program Manager, Division of Family Services, Department of Services for Children, Youth and Their Families, 1825 Faulkland Road, Wilmington, DE 19805; 302/633-2601.
** The contact person for the Casey Family Program is Ruth W. Massinga, Chief Executive Officer, Seattle, WA; 206/282-7300.

The Cuyahoga County START (Sobriety Treatment and Recovery Teams) Program

Having documented that 75% of child welfare intake involved alcohol and other drug abuse, officials in Cuyahoga County, Ohio, launched a program in 1996 that built on earlier AOD-targeted efforts to weave together the strengths of AOD treatment providers with the needs of child welfare families. The elements of the program are listed below:

- Expanded worker training in AOD issues;

- Random urinalysis as a motivation booster for parents in treatment;

- Safety plans that address AOD problems explicitly;

- Natural support providers and relatives;

- Referrals to four local AOD treatment agencies; and,

- An explicit message to clients that says...

> We want you to understand now, at the beginning, that permanent custody of your child will depend on this success. You must stop your drug use if you are going to have responsibility for your child [Cuyahoga County Department of Child & Family Services 1996].

The target group is the estimated 150 women a year who deliver babies and show a positive toxicology screen for any drug. A key feature of the program is the use of "child welfare advocates," who are recovering AOD abusers recruited from local welfare offices and past child welfare caseloads.

 The Sacramento County Alcohol and Other Drug Treatment Initiative (AODTI). In response to the flood of AOD cases in social service and public health caseloads, the Sacramento County Department of Health and Human Services enacted in 1993 an initiative to incorporate substance abuse services as an integral part of its service delivery systems. The program received full endorsement from the Sacramento County Board of Supervisors, the Human Services Cabinet, and the Criminal Justice Cabinet.

The training component of the initiative focused on three levels:

- Level I - Basic introduction to AOD terminology and identification,
- Level II - Advanced assessment and intervention skills including certification in administering the Substance Abuse Subtle Screening Inventory (SASSI), and
- Level III - Group treatment skills with substance-abusing clients.

Level I was required for *all* Department of Health and Human Services personnel. Level II was required for all personnel who "carry a caseload." Level III training was required for all County AOD counseling staff and was voluntary for all other staff who completed Level II and agreed to participate in facilitating AOD group services. The program's three levels of training had been completed by more than 2,000 health and human service staff members and other community agencies by early 1998. Sacramento currently requires that workers begin AOD training after their first three months on the job. (The lessons of this initiative are discussed in Chapter 3.) The training was evaluated with a pre- and post-training test that assessed participants' knowledge, attitudes, and beliefs. Post-training results showed considerable initial approval from line employees. The substantive areas of the training that produced the most positive responses to the pre- and post-training questions included the following:

- The awareness that alcoholism and drug dependence are diseases,
- The awareness that professionals can help clients in denial,
- The effectiveness of different modalities of treatment for different kinds of clients,
- The relevance of client measures of functioning in addition to abstinence,

- Alleviating the misapprehension that the AODTI sought to make all professionals into drug counselors,
- Definitions and symptoms of AOD dependence,
- The potential for all human service professionals to conduct substance abuse interventions, and
- Awareness of phases of recovery as measures of parents' readiness for child custody.

Overall, workers gave highly favorable scores on the questions: "I think this training will result in a change in how I do my job," "I will recommend to my coworkers that they participate in this training," and "I think that it is important that the department is undertaking this training program." An important distinction emerged, as it often does in training, among changes in *knowledge, attitudes,* and *expected versus observed behavior.* In answer to the question "as a result of this training, the primary change that I will make in the way I do my job is...," workers responded far more often "feel more knowledgeable in dealing with AOD problems" than they agreed with "be more understanding and sensitive to clients with AOD problems." The least frequent response was "be more willing to confront and talk about AOD problems," suggesting the greater difficulty of turning new attitudes into new practices.

At the peak of implementation, around January 1997, approximately two-thirds of all child welfare workers (outside the permanent placement bureau where parents have already been assessed for risk) were submitting AOD assessments. Later in 1997, the CPS crisis (see box on page 39) resulted in a reduction of assessments to a point where few were coming in from workers.

The actual procedure for AOD assessment and referral under the AODTI involved three steps:

1. Classifying the client (use of the SASSI was at workers' discretion as a tool to assist in this classification) as falling into one of five categories:

- Having no AOD problem,
- Substance user,

- Substance abuser,
- Chemically dependent not in recovery, or
- Chemically dependent in recovery.

2. Determining, among those clients assessed with an AOD-related problem, their level of functioning based on a Likert scale across seven domains that are commonly used in AOD assessment protocols:

- Medical problems,
- Social relationships,
- Legal problems,
- Housing problems,
- Mental health problems,
- Family problems, or
- Employment problems.

3. Referral to one or more of nine treatment options based on a grid that indicates appropriate patient placement guidelines for referrals to a continuum of treatment programs.

During the period in which assessments were at peak levels, 63% of all clients assessed were described as having an AOD problem at some level, with another 14% described as chemically dependent and in recovery. As a finding from the most comprehensive AOD assessment process systematically applied to all CWS-entering parents, this statistic correlates with many other national studies, which find 40 to 80% of CWS-involved parents have an AOD problem.

An important intervention developed as a part of the AODTI makes clear that the effort was designed and implemented as much more than a training program; this was the use of "pretreatment groups" run by social workers and/or AOD counselors. In contrast to a frequent CWS agency practice of referring clients with AOD problems to a "waiting list" at a treatment program (which some have derisively called "referral on demand" in contrast with the policy of *treatment* on demand), the AODTI used these pretreatment groups as a means of immediately engaging the clients who needed AOD treatment. Clients are involved in a group setting that includes parents with similar problems from whom they can receive support. In some cases, this may be the only intervention required. In the case of higher risk, lower functioning parents, the groups serve as interim services while waiting for an intensive treatment slot to open. Approximately one-third of AODTI clients with AOD problems were referred to such groups at the peak period of assessments.

The Sacramento CPS Crisis. With the deaths of two young children during 1996-97 whose parents were involved in drugs, the CWS agency within Sacramento County's Department of Health and Human Services became preoccupied with tougher enforcement. Under media pressure and criticisms from advocates for children, the district attorney's office, in collaboration with DHHS, the probation department, and law enforcement, conducted "sweeps" of neighborhoods to place children in protective custody. At one point in late 1997, the sweeps had increased the number of children "filed on," (i.e., on whom formal removal proceedings had begun in court) by seven times its normal rate in prior months. The AODTI assessment policy was suspended, and plans were implemented to reduce work loads as staff came under great pressure to remove children at risk, without devoting any resources to assessing their parents' AOD-related status. Submissions of AOD assessment forms dropped to very few by late 1997. By early 1998, a renewed effort to commit resources to a revised assessment process was under way.

The Pensacola Family Drug Court

After 15 years on the bench, Judge John Parnham has a vision of a Family-Focused Community Justice System. To achieve that vision, he has changed his approach in working with families with AOD-related problems and believes that the Dependency Court should serve the community as a form of "therapeutic jurisprudence, empowering families to be in a healthy environment." In a strong collaborative effort among the court; the district AOD program administrator, Dr. Paul Rollings; the district Family Safety and Preservation administration; and the staff at Pathways Treatment Center, the principles that have been used in adult criminal drug courts have been implemented in the family dependency court since 1997.*

The families brought into the drug court have generally had open cases in the Family Safety and Preservation Division for many years and have all been court-ordered to complete a treatment plan. Drug court families are from the family reunification and court-ordered family supervision programs. If the case worker finds that the family is not cooperating in their treatment plan and the parent(s) have AOD problems, the case is referred to the state attorney's office for filing contempt of court charges. The parent is ordered to appear in front of Judge Parnham and if the parent is in violation of the court order, has no psychiatric problems that would interfere with the treatment, and agrees to participate in the drug court services, the family can be accepted to the drug court program.

AOD treatment services are provided in four phases by Pathways, a local AOD treatment provider. Although there are timelines set for each phase, the time limits are flexible and adjusted for each client's progress in treatment. The phases of treatment are:

- *Phase 1.* 4 hours per day, 4 days per week for 5 weeks;

- *Phase 2.* 4 hours per day, 2 days per week for 3 to 6 months;

- *Phase 3.* 1 1/2 hours per day, 2 days per week for 6 months; and

- *Phase 4.* Long-term case management for approximately 6 months.

There are weekly court appearances and random selections for urine tests during Phase 1. Court appearances and drug testing is less frequent as the structure of the program becomes less rigorous over time.

Each member of the drug court team believes that the key component of its success is the emphasis on linkages among the partners.

---

* For additional information on the Pensacola Drug Court, contact Dr. Paul Rollings, Program Administrator, Florida Department of Children and Families Substance Abuse Program; 850/444-8366.

There are weekly case planning meetings in which each team member has a voice in reaching consensus on rewards and sanctions to be delivered under the authority of the court. Most important in case planning is the view from each perspective on the treatment team on the client's "patterns of behavior." Even if a client is testing clean, if the AOD counselor or CWS social worker believe that the client is not demonstrating a change in his/her behavior patterns, they can request the imposition of sanctions. Sanctions used by the court include more frequent court appearances, daily urine tests, community service jobs, and when necessary, jail time.

Putting the Models in Context

In summarizing the state of the art of CWS-AOD relations in 1992, the CWLA Commission at that time said

> Currently, the child welfare and AOD service systems operate independently from each other, using different eligibility criteria, restrictive funding streams, and sometimes conflicting program requirements, creating a maze that severely limits access [CWLA 1992].

Today, in 1998, the practices and policies in the exemplary agencies we have discussed in this chapter have advanced well beyond this summary description. We have made progress, despite the large obstacles that remain. The "maze that severely limits access" is still there, arguably more confusing because of new categorical legislation and the lack of adequate data collection.

But the recognition of the problem of AOD abuse by parents in the child welfare system is much wider than it was in the early 1990s. Demonstration programs, as noted in this section, have shown that advances in AOD treatment can make a difference in child welfare outcomes. The 1992 judgment of inadequate community response is still true of many communities, but practice innovation is expanding the number of child welfare agencies that are trying to break out of this status quo. We turn now to an assessment of child welfare innovation, as it provides further evidence of the progress that has been made.

Child Welfare Trends, Practice Innovations, and AOD-related Issues

Several recent trends and practice innovations in the child welfare field are closely related to the AOD problems addressed in this guidebook. Some are changes in child welfare practice that could result in more effective handling of AOD problems, but others may present barriers to closer links with AOD treatment agencies. The following material discusses these innovations as they influence and are influenced by AOD problems. Some of the common themes in these innovations and trends include *family-centered practice* and *strengths-based* or *solution-focused practice*. These approaches identify and build on the strengths of the families in the child welfare system, while recognizing that those strengths are challenged by the forces that cause and are affected by AOD abuse.

Kinship Care

While not a new innovation, kinship care has expanded in the past decade to a point where it makes up as much as one-half of new placements in some states and counties, and it can be seen as both a major resource and a challenge in weaving together AOD and CWS practice and policy. On the one hand, kinship care is undeniably a resource that has provided safe, loving homes for thousands of children whose parents were unable to care for them responsibly, due to their own AOD and other problems. As of 1994, approximately 2.15 million children–just over 3% of all children in the United States—were estimated to live in the care of relatives without a parent present [Harden et al. 1997]. Since "concurrent planning" (described on page 44) relies on kinship care as an early option, the use of this form of care is likely to increase rather than decrease in years ahead, as more restrictive time limits for both CWS and TANF begin to take hold.

At the same time, the intergenerational, genetic factors in AOD use and abuse, while not determinative, are highly correlative within families, and policy needs to take into account the possibility that the AOD issues may be present in the kinship setting in ways that can affect children. As Ivory Johnson has written, inadequate kinship care "can be another system of abuse and neglect for vulnerable children" [Johnson 1994]. The AOD issues in kinship arrangements are at least as important as they are in other caregivers' homes, and should be assessed as such. Johnson emphasizes that workers dealing with kinship arrangements

> must be skilled in family assessment to be able to understand the implications of chemical abuse and dependence on one's ability to provide adequate parenting and protection. The dynamics of chemical abuse and dependency must be part of the core training for kinship caregivers and staff members.

One recent assessment of kinship foster care based on a review of 77 cases underscored the difficulty of dealing with AOD issues when both the caregiver and the parent are experiencing AOD problems, as would be expected since they are both affected by the familial roots of AOD dependence [Gleeson et al. 1997]. The rationale for whole-family treatment is always strong, but addressing the intergenerational issues in kinship care is a special challenge, due to the greater likelihood that some of the underlying factors contributing to maltreatment could be present in the kinship setting as well as in the biological home. An especially difficult set of issues must be dealt with by caregivers and agency workers when birth parents are still actively abusing substances or are incarcerated [Crumbley & Little 1997].

The broad principles that appear to have the best chance of ensuring that kinship care will provide safe and supportive homes for children include the following:

- Screening and assessment of the families in sufficient depth to address AOD issues explicitly;

- Adequate resources for kinship families;

- A recognition by public policy and agency workers' practices that kinship care is different from family foster care and requires different services and supports; and

- Clarity about how kinship care and permanency planning interact, both in policy and in individual case planning.

Racial and cultural issues are deeply ingrained in kinship care and must be explicitly and sensitively addressed. As Johnson and many others note, "the kinship care arrangement is a practice rooted in the African and American experience" [Johnson 1994], and is of great importance in Native American communities as well.

Concurrent Planning

The goal of concurrent planning is *timely permanency for children*. In contrast with *sequential planning* (which seeks reunification and then, if these efforts prove unsuccessful, introduces alternative permanency plans), concurrent planning provides for parental reunification and rehabilitation efforts while simultaneously developing an alternative permanent plan for the child. An agency using concurrent planning methods simultaneously offers services to families while exploring alternative permanent options. The agency reviews relative/kinship placement options and seeks foster/adoption placement as a backup plan if reunification is not possible in 12 or 18 months. All options are discussed, including active rehabilitation efforts, voluntary relinquishment, and relative guardianship. Frequent, consistent, and meaningful visitation is used as a high predictor of reunification in concurrent planning. Concurrent planning for children and families requires caseload adjustments to reflect the more intensive level of services delivered by child welfare workers.

AOD problems are critical to concurrent planning, since the "fork in the road" often comes when the agency makes a decision about whether parents are able to resume their responsibility for their children. Some child welfare practitioners have expressed the view that AOD problems are in fact the most important barrier to making concurrent planning work. In their view, without adequate means of referring parents to treatment, monitoring their progress, and making a well-grounded assessment of the risk of returning children, concurrent planning cannot succeed.

The State of Colorado, for example, uses concurrent planning to make early decisions on families needing substance abuse services.

Concurrent Planning: Significance for AOD Issues

The pressure to deal with AOD issues increases when the "second track" of permanent placement outside the biological family is apparent from the start. Consistent with the goals of the 1997 federal legislation and some states' moves toward allowing shorter time periods for reunification services for parents with AOD problems, CWS agencies have accelerated their efforts to make judgments on AOD-abusing parents. But CWS practice may be unrealistic in assuming that a single episode of treatment will "fix" a parent with lifelong habits and a lifestyle in which AOD abuse may be only one manifestation of family problems.

Staff have new resources for AOD treatment slots and reduced caseloads that enable intensive reunification services combined with concurrent planning for adoption based on parental performance in treatment. At three months the case is reviewed and a recommendation is prepared for concurrent foster care or adoption. By six months, the agency feels it has adequate information from AOD treatment providers to determine whether reunification is likely and, if not, to accelerate termination of parental rights. "With few exceptions, permanent placements must be made by 12 months" [Barth 1997].

This speeding up of the "AOD clock" runs the risk that parents who need longer than 12 months to achieve parenting skills and personal stability will have lost their children by the time they get their lives together. But the alternative in this difficult set of choices is waiting for the parents, at an obvious cost to the children if the parents are not successful. In some cases, the CWS legal clock and the child's developmental clock will become a higher priority and may take precedence over the slower running AOD recovery clock.

Family Decision-Making Models

As documented in a recent publication of the American Humane Association, agencies have begun to use an approach to families called

---

**Family Decision-Making Models:
Significance for AOD Issues**

The skills required to facilitate a family's discussion of "undiscussable" issues that include AOD problems are not always present in CWS staffing. It is not clear whether facilitators consistently seek to assure, as AOD counselors sometimes do in arranging family-based interventions, "hearing the voices of those who have been victimized" and "holding those who have committed the wrong responsible for their actions," in the words of one presentation of FGDM.

Family Group Decision Making (FGDM), that emphasizes building on the strengths of families and using a solution-based approach to resolve family problems that may lead to out-of-home placement. This approach includes a family case conferencing model developed in New Zealand and the Family Unity Model developed in Oregon and based on the Family Group Conferencing model.

Both processes use family meetings as the central mechanism to develop a family resource plan, drawing on the resources of the family, the extended family, and community agencies. The family assumes responsibility for the plan and takes ownership of the steps needed to carry it out.

The Family Unity Model uses a trained facilitator to assist the extended family unit in developing the family resource plan. In the Family Group Conferencing model, a facilitator provides initial guidance to the family but the family develops the plan, with the facilitator leaving the room when the extended family deliberations are under way.

These models are quite appealing in the reduced intrusiveness they bring to families' lives and their ability to hold families accountable for their own actions. They also offer an approach that is effective with diverse cultural groups. A further advantage pointed out by some state officials is that FGDM models create a team for the worker to be part of, which can be a welcome support for a younger, less experienced worker who no longer needs to make all decisions by herself.

While there is not as yet a significant body of evidence about the effectiveness of these models, the combination of an approach that is more respectful of clients and provides workers more resources has led a number of states and counties to adopt FGDM. As with concurrent planning, however, some practitioners would caution that implementing these approaches with social workers assigned their current levels of caseloads will not be successful. It remains to be seen if these added resources will be made available.

The Family Support Movement

Some of the programmatic and philosophical underpinnings of the community partnerships approach are firmly rooted in earlier ideas about family support, building on family strengths, the need for natural supports as well as public and nonprofit services, and respect for the cultural and community origins of families. Securing support from the community in helping parents in the CWS system is at the core of the community partnership approach.

Some documents produced by the family support movement have given AOD issues scant attention, but the field as a whole varies widely in the depth of its approach to AOD concerns. Yet there is extensive evidence that self-help approaches, both neighborhood-based and faith-based, can help families both in early intervention and in community-based aftercare support from networks of natural helpers that include other parents in recovery. In addressing the issue of whether a strengths-based approach makes it difficult to address a family's AOD problems, some practitioners would agree with the statement by one reviewer that

> ... In no case do we view "family strengths" as an approach that ignores needs—rather it is an approach that uses family and personal resources, successes, and capabilities as essential components of creating plans to successfully address *needs* such as AOD, violence reductions, improved parenting, etc. [Anonymous communication with author, 1998].

It is not difficult to see the conceptual links between family support practice and increased community involvement in AOD issues.

Two of the core principles of family support, as set forth in a series of publications by the Family Resource Coalition of America, are especially relevant. If one defines "having control over important aspects of their lives" and "equitable access to resources in the community" to include addressing AOD problems as they affect millions of children, the family support movement can become an important part of the effort to strengthen community support to parents with AOD problems [Family Resource Coalition 1996].

Another source of family support is the **school-linked services** movement. Services for AOD-related problems among parents have been included in several efforts: in Florida's statewide efforts to develop "full-service schools," and in statewide efforts in New Jersey, Kentucky, and California. These initiatives go well beyond the pilot project stage to widespread innovations in which public and community workers are brought into and linked with schools in family resource centers.

A specific form of family support program is **home visiting**. In an increasing number of communities, home visiting programs have been linked to child welfare reforms. Lawrence Sherman's extensive survey of crime reduction programs for the U.S. Department of Justice included a review of "family-based prevention" initiatives such as home visiting, and concluded:

> Perhaps the most promising results in all areas of crime prevention are found in the evaluations of home visitation programs. While these findings are often combined with other institutional elements, such as preschool, there is a large and almost uniformly positive body of findings on this practice [Sherman et al. 1997].

Home visiting programs have at times included counseling and treatment for AOD problems, especially those that are revealed by a positive toxicological screen at birth. But many programs have emphasized referral out to treatment agencies rather than equipping line staff to screen or provide pretreatment services.

References

Barth, R. (October 28, 1997). Substance abuse and child welfare: Problems and proposals. Testimony before the Subcommittee on Human Resources, Committee on Ways and Means, U.S. House of Representatives.

Center for the Study of Social Policy. (1997). *Strategies to keep children safe: Why community partnerships will make a difference.* Washington DC: Author.

Child Welfare League of America. (1992). *Children at the front: A different view of the war on alcohol and drugs.* Washington, DC: Author.

Crumbley, J., & Little, R. (Eds.). (1997). *Relatives raising children: An overview of kinship care.* Washington, DC: Author.

Cuyahoga County Department of Child and Family Services. (1996). *S.T.A.R.T.—Sobriety treatment and recovery teams.* Cleveland, OH: Author.

Family Resource Coalition. (1996). *Guidelines for family support practice.* Chicago, IL: Author.

Gleeson, J. P., O'Donnel, J., & Bonecutter, F. J. (1997). Understanding the complexity of practice in kinship foster care. *Child Welfare, 76,* 801-826.

Harden, A. W., Clark, R. C., & Maguire, K. (1997). *Informal and formal kinship care.* Washington, DC: U.S. Department of Health and Human Services, Office of the Assistant Secretary for Planning and Evaluation.

Johnson, I. L. (1994). Kinship care. In D. Besharov (Ed.), *When drug addicts have children.* Washington, DC: American Enterprise Institute and Child Welfare League of America.

Sherman, L. W., Gottfredson, D., MacKenzie, D., Eck, J., Reuter, P., & Bushway, S. (1997). *Preventing crimes: What works, what doesn't, what's promising.* Washington, DC: National Institute of Justice.

3

Lessons of the Models

The preceding discussion of the models and innovations that have been developed to respond to the problem of AOD abuse among child welfare clients reveals nine common themes. These themes provide lessons from the many attempts to improve the links between AOD and child welfare systems.*

Lesson #1
Values matter, especially when the issues touch AOD and poverty.

Our attitudes about drug use (and use of alcohol, the consequences of which are often much more serious) and poverty are among the most stereotyped topics in our society. As a result, the public debate on these subjects tends to lurch from extreme to extreme, rarely confronting the "gray areas" where difficult decisions are necessary. The public and its opinion leaders exhibit polar extremes of reaction and overreaction to "crises" that become media-visible and then fade. From

---

* This section owes a great deal to three authors (whose works have been disseminated and supported by the Annie E. Casey Foundation): Lisbeth Schorr in the United States, and Gerald Smale and John Brown in Great Britain, whose work has been published by the National Institute of Social Work (NISW). There is a rich set of literature on policy and program implementation in the United States, notably work done during the past 25 years that began with Wildavsky and Pressman's seminal *Implementation* in 1973. Schorr, Smale, and Brown have all built from this earlier work, renewing it and giving it special relevance for policy aimed at children and families. Schorr's new book *Common Purpose* is a follow-up work to her 1988 book, *Within Our Reach*, and addresses the problem of taking successful pilot projects to scale. Smale and Brown's work has been undertaken as part of the Managing Change and Innovation Programme of the NISW. See Brown, J. (1996). *Chance favours the prepared mind.* London: National Institute for Social Work. With the exception of Brown's title, quotes from Brown and Smale have been Americanized in spelling.

denial that there is a problem, attitudes then shift toward a crisis mentality in which expensive "quick fixes" are attempted.

At the same time, we compartmentalize our attitudes about these difficult issues. This is shown by the widespread inability to see the connection between socially acceptable drug use (e.g., caffeine, nicotine, alcohol, prescription drugs) and drug "abuse." The public equates drug abuse with the use of "hard drugs" by low-income persons, rather than the abuse of alcohol or the misuse of mood-altering drugs by middle- and upper-income persons.

In CWS-AOD reform, these attitudes can make it difficult to sustain public support for middle-ground reforms. In a number of communities, the debate about "zero-tolerance" policies that insist on abstinence for CWS clients is almost solely focused on illegal substances, ignoring the far greater impact of alcohol on child and family problems. This has made it difficult to realistically discuss the financial costs and psychological impacts of strictly enforcing such policies by removing all children from homes where parents are using drugs.

In Sacramento, a public discussion of the merits of "harm reduction" as a public policy toward AOD use was made more difficult following incidents of children's deaths in substance-abusing families. The results included removal of a much greater number of children from their homes, foster care cost increases in the millions of dollars, and expansion of out-of-county placements. The lesson appears to be that discussing such value-laden issues in noncrisis times may build a residue of public understanding, while discussing these issues in crisis environments is far more difficult.

We are overdue for a reasoned debate about what we mean by "harmful drug abuse" in the context of children and families. But that will require sustained policy leadership above the level of specific programs. No one program can alter public attitudes built up over decades and entrenched in a context created by centuries of public opinion underlying some of these issues. This lesson can also be stated as a recognition that the *context* of reform matters as much as its *content*.

Clarifying the values of the general public and key stakeholders is an important part of innovation and its marketing. But our reluctance to discuss values issues, and our tendency to polarize the debate when we do, complicates the values dimension of public education and policy change. What then happens is that in the absence of values consensus, policymakers and implementors tend to try to please everyone by "fudging" on the values choices: Which clients will get priority? When will sanctions be applied for clients who aren't in compliance? What is the role of the neighborhood in setting norms? These questions are values questions, but if innovation is carried on in an atmosphere that seems to be overly concerned with technical, fiscal, or programmatic issues, then the values issues will slip away and these questions will never be addressed in depth.

Targeting is an area where values matter a great deal. The decisions about whether male inmates or female parents should receive priority for limited AOD funding is not a technical decision—it is a values choice. And as we have already noted, whatever official policy statements may say about the importance of women and children, only 27% of publicly funded treatment slots are currently allocated to women.

Similarly, the decisions about when to terminate a parent's custody rights are obviously values decisions, and neither the laws or rules of program decision making will ever "automatically" force a decision to terminate parental rights. But in program design, as well as in implementation, these targeting decisions are often the last ones made. Often, they are made only by default, as events press for inclusion of one group, with the result that fewer of another group can be served unless funding is expanded. The targeting choices of how to respond to harder-to-serve clients are especially difficult, and programs usually opt out of these debates by taking a tacit position of "first come (or first referred), first served"—which is in effect saying the more difficult to serve will *not* be served.

Values disagreements are also important in negotiating the differences between CWS and AOD agencies, since each begins from different philosophical bases. The role of clients' motivation, the desire for abstinence in contrast with the need for harm reduction, the benefits of time limits and sanctions, the definition of client as parent, child, or whole family—these are just a few of the values issues that arise in serious dialogue between the two systems. None of these, in our view, is irreconcilable. But few will be addressed seriously enough to identify and work out the differences if the values issues are ruled out or ignored.

For that reason, we urge that a *collaborative values inventory* (see Appendix A) be used as a means of anonymously assessing the extent of consensus in a group working on AOD issues. A group may be trying to collaborate without ever discussing the major underlying values that may unite them—or divide them. This tool has helped some groups understand what their disagreements are about.

LESSON #2

Without early, strategic attention to the scope and scale of reform, innovation reverts to isolated, categorical pilot projects with little impact on the organization or the larger target population.

Innovation that "succeeds" at the level of a pilot project but does not move beyond that state to wider implementation is a failed innovation. Gerald Smale has developed a devastating critique of the pilot project mentality, arguing that "pilot projects are how an agency inoculates itself against change":

> Special projects can attract considerable resentment from others in the mainstream of the organization, especially if the project workers are released from statutory duties or given extra resources....*organizations can be inoculated against innovation.* While people on pilot projects are developing their new form of practice, others in the organization are working out how they are going to avoid working in the same way....No matter how much we learn from pilot projects, we need other strategies for disseminating results and achieving widespread change [Smale 1996: pp. 25-26].

In our own work, we have emphasized the frequency with which pilot projects ignore the real resources and exhibit a "Willie Sutton problem." Willie Sutton, a bank robber in the 1920s, was once asked why he kept robbing banks; his answer was supposedly, "That's where the money is." But in many communities, the emphasis is placed on relatively small, grant-funded pilot projects and on newly launched collaboratives, rather than changes in use of the much larger resources *already in the community* in the budgets of existing institutions.

Smale believes this pilot project mentality creates a barrier to innovation:

> ...departments are inoculated against innovation...[when] it is assumed that practice has changed after new management prescriptions have been declared, brief training undertaken, and the best intentions of staff have been gained [Smale 1996: p. 29].

He criticizes cursory training as the fallacy that "to know is to act differently." He also points out that reorganizing is how many organizations inoculate themselves against innovation; the reorganization itself is cited as though it were real change, and thus reduces the pressures for making real change at the frontline of practice. Weiner and others have also noted the tendency of organizations' political leaders to prefer to change *structure* rather than *strategy* when the organization comes under criticism [Weiner 1982].

Lisbeth Schorr agrees, using the phrase "the hidden ceiling on scale" to refer to barriers to expanding model projects. She suggests that effective replications share six attributes:

- They combine replicating the essence of a successful intervention with the adaptation of many of its components to a new setting.

- They have had the continuous backing of an intermediary organization.

- They recognize the importance of the systems and institutional context (i.e., they have an agenda for redirection of current resources, not just a grants agenda).

- They recognize the importance of the people context, requiring buy-in from line staff.

- They use a results-based outcomes orientation to judge success.

- They tackle, directly and strategically, the obstacles to large-scale change [Schorr 1997].

Using these criteria, it is possible to review pilot projects and distinguish those that have a solid chance of becoming strategic from those that are just isolated projects. For example, the CPS reform efforts in Missouri that have been implemented as a pilot project since 1994 included a built-in evaluation effort, were outcomes-driven, included more than 20% of the state's children in the demonstration areas, and proposed gradual phase-in of the features that proved effective. These elements gave far more assurance that the legislature and executive branch in Missouri were not just creating one more project, but were testing a model that had clear statewide implications from the first [Christian 1997].

It is obvious that sometimes legislators will adopt a pilot project when they could not be persuaded to take the greater risk of operating an innovation at a greater scale. In these cases, administrators seeking innovation have to weigh the costs and potential benefits of a pilot approach, including the likelihood that the legislature will accept evidence of success as a basis for expanding the innovation (as well as its readiness to support an adequate evaluation effort to document the outcomes). But it is the absence of a multiyear strategy and the tendency of some legislatures to spawn a series of unrelated pilot initiatives that justify caution in seeing a legislature's typical approach to pilot projects as a victory for innovation.

Some of these choices about the scale and structure of an innovation are visible in the choices made about how to organize the reform effort. One of the key choices is whether to place it at the core of the organization, to set it up as a separate unit removed from the mainstream of the organization's life, or to negotiate some compromise between these two poles. The trade-offs are clear: placing reform "all the way inside" the agency permits close ties to the organization's senior managers, but comes with the inevitable costs of moving at a slower pace acceptable to those managers. Placing the reform unit farther outside in a "sheltered" position enables greater flexibility and a faster moving style of operation, but may make it more difficult to work closely with the senior managers.

C A S E In Sacramento, the AODTI effort was placed in a "reform unit," separate from the CWS manag-**S T U D Y** ers who controlled the daily operations of the agency. But the leaders of the reform were chosen for their knowledge of the agency, with the ability to work with top managers and with line staff and community organizations. Until the CPS crisis created an entirely new situation, the reform unit had proven its ability to carry out Director Caulk's original vision and to mobilize resources throughout the agency for a "training-plus" reform that directly affected more than 2,000 employees of the agency who went through the training.

One reform manager noted that decisions about where to place an innovation unit were similar to decisions about quality assurance units, which need both independence to be able to judge effectiveness of agency practices and access to the mainstream of the organization to be credible. This tension and balancing is built into the decision about organizing reform, and knowing the organizational style and culture of an agency can help leaders make the right trade-offs in deciding how to structure reform so that model projects are not isolated.

Another arena that affects the scale of reform are the choices made about partnerships with external agencies. Operating from the basic premise that CWS reform requires resources *outside* the child welfare agency itself, supporters of any initiative that focuses on the impact of alcohol and other drugs must decide early how broadly to address the connections with the health and mental health system, the juvenile justice and adult corrections system, and the role of the courts. Some CWS reforms have started completely within the CWS agency, while others, including Sacramento's AODTI, have from the outset aimed their efforts more broadly at a wider array of targets.

 The Sacramento innovation team felt that their work with county criminal justice agencies and probation staff made it possible for them to carry the principles of the AODTI into other agencies and move beyond the child welfare arena of reform. "We were always more than CPS, from the start," stated one staff member.

This lesson about scale also relates to how a reform unit responds to the opportunities it has to influence other priorities of the organization *outside* the boundaries of the reform itself. This is related to the issue of parallel reforms discussed above. For example, in the past year, some CWS-AOD reform units have been forced to make a decision about how they are going to respond to welfare reform. Knowing that some of their clients will be directly affected by time limits, work requirements, and drug testing, CWS staffs have begun negotiations with TANF agencies. The temptation for some has been to "do another pilot," in which a small number of AOD treatment slots is set aside for TANF parents. But this approach may have the effect of restricting the scale of the reform to those few clients, instead of working directly with the TANF planning unit to set up new procedures and priorities for all TANF clients needing AOD services. Reformers need to recognize when they are achieving real system reform and when they have merely launched a new project that is buffered from the rest of the organization and unlikely to affect mainstream practice.

Finally, the issue of scale in reform is reflected in choices made about *rules*. In another context, we have used a four-stage theory of collaborative development that moves from earlier information exchange and joint projects to a third phase of *changing the rules* and a final stage of *changing the system* [Gardner, forthcoming]. In innovation, it is possible to distinguish between changes that take place *within* the rules of a given system, and those that seek to *change* the rules of the system. Clearly, the second kind of changes are harder, since they change relationships as well as rules [Smale 1996: p. 77]. The first involves changes in tasks and methods, while the second involves changes in roles and relationships as well. When roles and relationships are involved, innovation takes even more negotiation and buy-in from those whose roles will change, as we discuss in Lesson #6 (page 66).

In CWS-AOD linkages, roles are often at the core of proposed changes, and as a result, changes in assessment and referral practices feel to workers as if they are major disruptions in the rules of doing business. That is why out-stationing an AOD counselor in a CPS agency or a school is much less threatening than proposing to change the role of *all* of the AOD counselors in working with external agencies. With a pilot approach to decentralization, the organization seeks to build a buffer against change by the rest of the organization. It is safer for the organization than a large-scale change in roles—but much less effective because it involves only a single staff member.

Lesson #3
Reforming systems demand a "theory of resources."

Several of the models and innovations described in this guidebook (and several that we recommend in conclusion) require more resources; for example, expanding training, addressing the treatment needs of adolescents as well as parents, and achieving realistic caseloads do not occur without cost. Some models involve additions of more staff and more treatment slots, which also require more resources. In addition to greater resources, however, *better* services and *different* ways of working together are needed in both CWS and AOD agencies.

A multifaceted resource strategy is a critical prerequisite to getting out of the pilot project trap. In program evaluation, the concept of a "theory of change" has become an accepted way of examining the logic that connects an intervention and its intended outcomes. But we believe that a "theory of resources" is equally important in making clear the assumptions about how the reform can expand—answering the simple, loaded question: *Who would pay for more of it, if it works?*

Providing more resources to the current staff and agency leadership in most CWS and AOD agencies *to work the way they are currently working* would result in marginal changes at best. More staff would be available, but they would work in systems that would still be largely isolated, with increased referrals going back and forth between them but without agreements on new assessments to ensure that clients end up in programs that have the best chance of helping them. Workers unwilling or unable to ask the critical questions about AOD problems will miss as many cases as the current system, even if there are more workers. Nor will new funding provide any guarantees that progress will be made by AOD and CWS providers working under current purchase-of-services contracts, as long as those contracts measure success by numbers treated rather than according to the success rates and characteristics of the clients in the caseloads.

As noted above in discussing treatment effectiveness, not all parents need 18-month residential programs to be able to deal with their AOD problems. It is totally beyond the realm of fiscal possibility to replicate existing model programs across the entire system with intensive funding—*and a large percentage of parents don't need such intensive treatment for that length of time.* Generalizing from a "Cadillac program" is a fallacy of demonstration program thinking, assuming that if an intensive program works for some clients it will work for all and is needed by all.

In AOD-CWS reforms, four elements of a resource strategy are essential:

- *Savings and cost avoidance.* The data cited in this report on cost-effectiveness make a powerful case that treatment for the families and adolescents who are most at risk will have a payoff for those clients who complete treatment. Agencies need to commit resources to continuing to verify that the results of better AOD-CWS links can be proven cost effective, as the only way to justify budget decisions to move resources from the higher cost programs such as criminal justice and residential care to earlier treatment and prevention efforts. This strategy is currently being used in a number of mental health and juvenile diversion programs, such as in Alameda County, California, where more expensive slots for out-of-home care have been diverted to earlier intervention. Home visiting for high-risk parents and infants is another arena in which this principle of cost avoidance has been put to work.

- *Redirection of funding from ineffective programs.* The argument for new funding rests implicitly on a premise that existing programs are effective. This premise cannot always be proven, and in fact has been disproved in some critical AOD and CWS programs, including school-based prevention programs (e.g., DARE). The great majority of parent education programs, an intervention used frequently for CWS clients, do not measure the outcomes of their instruction, but simply monitor attendance, with a few using pre- and post-tests that assess what parents *say* they are doing differently. In one community of 300,000 in which we work, there were four years ago 63 separate parent education programs—only a small number of which even used pre- and post-testing to determine their effectiveness. Until results-based accountability is applied intensively to programs to help parents or prevent risky behavior by adolescents, it is inaccurate to assume that new funding for these programs will invariably produce better results.

- *Blended funding.* The National Center for Child Abuse and Neglect demonstration projects mentioned earlier concluded that providing "collaborative, not categorical funding opportunities" was one of the most important policy changes that could be made in strengthening CWS-AOD links. The extraordinary efforts made by intensive services programs in some cities, securing funding from as many as 40 different funding sources, have come at a cost of countless hours of overhead time devoted to grant chasing and multiple reporting requirements. Blended funding legislation in a number of states has begun to encourage communities to develop "bottom-up block grants" by allowing agencies more discretion to combine categorical funds in return for specified outcomes.

- *Mobilize people resources at the community level.* Finally, a theory of resources has to recognize that there are many more important resources than public funding. The "people power" and natural helping networks available in a community that understands and supports AOD-CWS goals can provide valuable citizen energy that multiples staff time greatly. Mobilizing this kind of citizen energy is what the Community Partnership approaches have been trying to do in the sites mentioned above, and it represents a serious resource strategy that can be far more valuable than securing another demonstration grant that runs out in three to five years. Faith-based organizations have often provided this kind of resource by donating their facilities for organizations of recovering persons, providing shelter for homeless AOD clients, and assisting with aftercare supports through networks of church members and outreach efforts.

To summarize this lesson about resources, there was an instructive incident in a recent session with federal grantees who were reaching the end of their five-year funding cycle. In a group of staff members from these programs, all of which provide AOD treatment to women with children, one grantee said in response to a presentation on funding options and sustainability strategies: "Why weren't we given this in the first year instead of the fifth year?"

That is the heart of our critique of pilot projects–not that they have not accomplished a great deal to show how systems can be changed, but that they typically lack (and funders have not sufficiently encouraged them to develop) a strategic conception of how to build on their successes with a theory of resources, a redirection agenda, and an institutionalization plan. Projects that have achieved success deserve more than mere refunding with another grant; they deserve sustained support in working to transfer their progress to wider levels of implementation.

Lesson #4

Parallel reforms and external crises can reinforce or undermine innovation.

In many communities, multiple innovations are under way as part of education reform, welfare reform, community development, youth services, Goals 2000, community asset mapping, substance abuse prevention, etc. In some neighborhoods, multiple decentralized facilities have been established, representing both public agencies and nonprofit or community-based organizations. At times, these initiatives compete with each other for publicity, elected officials' support, volunteers, grants, and other resources. In some cases, however, CWS-AOD reform has been able to make strong connections with AOD prevention campaigns, welfare reform, family resource centers, and county decentralized operations. Being aware of these parallel reforms is the first step toward avoiding competition as much as possible and achieving optimum impact whenever that is possible.

C A S E In Sacramento, a matrix was developed that listed all the decentralized, community-based initiatives **S T U D Y** serving children and families. As this was being compiled, staff working on it were told that no such matrix of all neighborhood initiatives had ever been developed, and were asked to send copies to virtually everyone surveyed in its development. When completed, it showed dozens of separate offices sponsored by different city, school, county, state, and federal programs—none of which had ever been included in an effort to rationalize these programs in a single area. As a result, an early priority for the decentralization of CPS activities in two neighborhoods was clarifying their relationships to other decentralized initiatives already in these areas.

Some practitioners would point out that when an organization is already in the midst of innovation, (e.g., implementing welfare reform or a new child welfare information system), it is not a good time to launch new, *parallel reforms* that may compete with the prior innovation. As one organizational theorist notes, there is an obvious paradox: sometimes "we are too busy changing to look at how we are managing innovation and change" [Smale 1996: p. 77].

Sometimes crisis becomes the only external force that matters. In the CWS arena, by definition, the death or serious injury of a child becomes a spotlight event that can radically change perceptions of the agency and its workers and leaders. Once a critical incident throws a spotlight on an agency, major changes can result. As noted in Sacramento, this meant a seven-fold increase in the number of children whose parents were cited for substantiated abuse or neglect. Such an increase in caseloads and removals of children meant that normal operating styles were suspended in the short run in favor of new processes designed to err on the side of child safety. As a result, new AOD assessments became, ironically, an assignment that workers avoided, even though AOD problems were causing such an increase in caseloads.

Some studies of innovation argue that innovation works best when times are "normal" and resources are not overly tight, enabling changes to be made with transitional support for those workers and other stakeholders who will bear the main brunt of the innovation. The alternative theory is that innovation works best in times of crisis when an organization can do extraordinary things under the pressure of external events, creating a team spirit that mobilizes new resources and new energy. Only a local team can judge which of these is a more accurate reading of the local reality at any given point. In some sites, however, a CWS crisis that temporarily overshadowed AOD-related reforms eventually reinforced the *need for the reform*, once policy leaders understood that AOD issues and their fiscal effects were unavoidable.

Lesson #5

Leadership matters.

Leadership is important to innovation in several ways. First, leadership in innovation matters because leaders change over time; such changes can be beneficial or disruptive. But the deeper into the organization the reform goes, the more likely it can survive transition after leadership changes. So one task of leaders is to ensure that the roots of the innovation grow as deep as possible.

Leaders greatly influence innovation through their choices of the people who will carry out innovations on a day-to-day basis. Thus, staffing is one of the most important processes in reforming a system, since these are the people who will seek to bend the system to the new ways of doing business and, at times, to confront the system about its need to change. The skills and attitudes of these implementors become the critical ingredients of reform, determining the pace, intensity, and resources available to the innovation. The most fateful choices in innovation often are leaders' selection of their key subordinates, which becomes a form of succession planning for the initiative, if not the entire organization.

Second, leadership matters because leaders, at their best, articulate a vision and then guide a team in a clear set of actions that carries out the vision. As the innovation goes into action, the important part of the vision becomes the *accountability* for carrying it out—developing measures of progress and taking them seriously by using them to ensure that key supervisors are "on board" and not subverting the innovation. Experience in several innovations suggests that it is definitely not micromanaging for an innovation leader to monitor his or her priority initiatives to make sure that they are supported by key managers and line staff. Once those managers have been given a clear explanation of the problem, the logic behind the solution, and an opportunity to become active in designing the innovation, if their behavior remains blocking or subversive, they have become part of the problem and should be moved to other, less critical assignments.

 The importance of leadership is apparent in the observation made by Dr. Robert Caulk in 1993, the Director of Sacramento County's Department of Health and Human Services; he stated that AOD was "almost 100% of our intake," forcing a "paradigm shift." In Caulk's lexicon, that meant that *all* HHS workers had to deal with AOD issues, and thus all should be adequately trained in doing so. Caulk's role was as a classic "product champion," to use a phrase from the innovation literature, which connotes a major top-level policy or management official who frames and defends the innovation. Not all of his mid-level supervisors were "on board" with the new view of AOD issues, and some who were in critical positions had to be replaced before the project could move beyond the training-only trap.

Third, leaders have to get the resources needed for innovation by selling it to their own leaders: the elected officials or senior management generalists who control resources. Director Caulk's efforts to keep the County Chief Administrative Officer and the Board of Supervisors supportive of the AODTI were major accomplishments in the early stages of the innovation, and the loss of that support once the CPS crisis (ensuing from the tragic deaths of two children who had been under CPS oversight) became visible and slowed the reform brought a major shift in the resources available to the effort.

Lesson #6

Successful innovation actively involves people in the organization, especially those whose work is the focus of the innovation.

This lesson deals with worker buy-in, shared definitions of a problem, and the value of a deliberate process of "mapping" the support needed to achieve real reform. The primary point is that *selling the problem is a prerequisite to selling a solution.* If planning and innovation occur without "selling the problem" to all of the workers in the agency, the innovation will slip to a lesser priority when the agency is faced with a crisis.

C A S E
S T U D Y "We agreed on the solution before we agreed on the problem" was how one staff member of Sacramento's CWS reform described the difficulty of persuading line staff that abuse of alcohol and other drugs was a central problem that required new training, new assessment tools, and a new way of operating with families. As self-evident as the AOD problem may appear, it does not automatically ensure implementation of the changes in daily practice required if an agency takes the AOD problem seriously. This issue is especially important in responding to the challenges of winning support from staff and managers.

Smale suggests that implementing innovation is a process of thinking clearly about three questions:

- Who sees what as a problem?

- What needs to change?

- What should stay the same? [Smale 1996: pp. 48-53]

We use these three questions to assess Sacramento County's initiative as a case study to illuminate what the Sacramento AODTI implementors tried to carry out as the priority goals, while pointing out some of the problems that were encountered in implementation.

C A S E
S T U D Y
"Who sees what as a problem" in Sacramento's AODTI? Smale's first question, "Who sees what as a problem?" was answered primarily by the planners of the AODTI, who saw the absence of AOD training as a problem for effective CPS practice. Careful monitoring of line workers' attitudes was also attempted through consultation efforts and the pre- and post-training survey of workers' responses to the training. But when the CPS crisis hit, it seems fair to say that workers and their supervisors did not see the AODTI and its new assessment options as a solution to their problem, but as a new problem itself. The lack of adequate buy-in from supervisors and managers meant that these supervisors did not have any attachment to the AODTI as an innovative approach that addressed a problem they felt to be significant enough to require new training and new assessments. Despite serious and ongoing efforts to involve both line workers and their supervisors, a majority of both groups essentially abandoned the AODTI when the pressures of the deaths of two children in the system created a new reality in the problem of rapidly expanding caseloads. The innovation had become the problem, not a solution to a larger problem accepted by both the innovators and the implementors.

To apply the concept of seeing innovation as the solution to a problem, the leaders of the Sacramento AODTI viewed the problem as the fact that AOD-related problems were affecting "nearly 100%" of clients in the Department of Health and Human Services. This seemed overwhelmingly obvious: the numbers showed it, intake studies showed it, experience in other states and cities showed it. The solution, consisting of training, new assessments, and a new referral mechanism, was developed by managers at the top level of the organization, in consultation with line workers. The innovation was delivered by a combination of inside and outside staff and consultants, and was accepted by line workers and supervisors (until the external pressure of the CPS crisis).

As Smale puts it, "To introduce 'solutions' to people who do not perceive themselves as having a problem will not unreasonably be seen as imposing a gratuitous burden, or at least an inconvenient interruption in their work...It is unhelpful to focus on the innovation alone and judge success only in terms of the adoption or application of the innovation. It is dangerous if the innovation becomes a cause in its own right" [Smale 1996: p. 40].

At this point, innovation may be reinforced if the organization has adopted an approach to results-based accountability that emphasizes the *outcomes* of innovation, rather than the process of its implementation. If the innovation is seen as a solution to a measurable problem, results-based accountability will seek both *client and system outcomes* that track progress toward solving the problem.

Therefore, the number of staff trained is far less important as a useful measure of progress than *what they do differently when they return to carrying out the daily practices of the organization*. Sacramento monitored both kinds of outcomes, and one of the clearest signals that the innovation was not going well was when staff submissions of client assessments for AOD problems did not keep pace with the number of new cases in the system.

C A S E **S T U D Y** "What needs to change" in Sacramento's AODTI? In turning to the "What needs to change?" question, the reality of daily practice must be stressed: *line workers are the key to daily practice reform*. Their support for the changes in daily practice required for the innovation is critical to moving from a vision to change to making the change. Nor should workers be seen as inherently opposed to reform, if the reform is presented carefully after consultation with line workers' representatives. A recent publication prepared by staff of the AFL-

CIO and funded by the Annie E. Casey Foundation described several examples of union-supported human services reform [Calicchia & Ginsburg 1996].

In CWS practice, paperwork and the role of supervisors are both vital to influencing what line workers actually do. Substantial amounts of paperwork are inherent in CWS, because legal mandates compel a paper trail of what has happened to the client and whether time limits have been met. Supervisors, in turn, are where line workers go for advice (and for shared responsibility) in dealing with the hardest cases. In normal times, an increase in paperwork and mandates for new procedures will be unwelcome. In times when caseloads have increased, workers are even more insistent that their time be protected. In such times, if new forms are mandated, they may be filled out and submitted to adhere to rules, but they will not be thoroughly done or be useful as trustworthy data. If they are optional, few workers will comply.

C A S E S T U D Y In Sacramento, where the CPS crisis led to a dramatic decline in workers submitting required assessment forms, it was clear that the union was not opposed to the AOD training and assessments as such, but to the "layering" of new paperwork requirements and the new assessment *on top of* existing paperwork, which increased the time it took to fill out the new forms at a time when caseloads and pressures on workers were increasing greatly. (Added complexity resulted when the new AOD assessment process came during a period in which a new state CWS information system was being implemented, as well as a proposed state pilot risk assessment system.)

Some students of human services reform argue that mapping change requires identifying who, if any, are the perceived *victims* of the innovation. "Whose identity is changed?" is one way they phrase this question that has special relevance for CWS-AOD linkages [Smale 1996]. In such initiatives across CWS and AOD systems, an effort is being made to get both sets of professionals to work more effectively with the other system, in ways that sometimes appear to threaten workers' sense of their own identity. (It did not help in one of these initiatives when a senior official stated to the media that all CWS workers would become AOD counselors, confirming many of their suspicions about role change that had already been voiced.) Innovation threatens the sense of identity of AOD workers who are told that they need to understand the child welfare system, and, similarly, of CWS workers who are told that they need to understand a completely different AOD treatment system.

Supervisors' reactions to new policy and changes in practice will determine a great deal of the response of line workers. The line workers carry out the daily practice of an agency, but key resource decisions are made by their senior managers—the directors and deputy directors of AOD and CPS agencies. In reforms where any of these key officials are lukewarm or opposed to the reform, their lack of support can cause costly delays in implementation. A senior manager who does not agree with an innovation has dozens of daily opportunities to overtly send that message to lower level staff, and line staff will quickly recognize such opposition.

Gaining the support of top managers is an important element in the initial phases of reform. When the goal is adapting to changes that raise the priority given to AOD problems, the whole organization must understand and accept these changes, and senior managers can set the tone for the acceptance. Whether those managers are in central offices or leading community-based decentralized teams, they can provide protection for innovation-minded staff who will otherwise wait until they get strong signals from their supervisors before they agree to take the risks of innovative practice. Sometimes senior managers who are working at the neighborhood level can effectively counter innovation blockers in the central office, but only if they are skilled leaders who understand how to help line staff adapt to change.

A further lesson that bears upon the role of senior managers is that training aimed solely at line workers may omit some management training needed by more senior staff who are expected to lead reform, but who may themselves not understand (or agree with) either its rationale or the new techniques being advocated. Staff development for senior managers of an agency is at least as important as training for line workers, but it can be much more difficult to arrange the time and ensure the credibility of the training aimed at senior

---

Beyond Training to Changing the Rules

This lesson reinforces two points made earlier in this document:

- The crucial role of assessment in tying together CWS and AOD efforts, and
- The failure of training alone to achieve system reform.

Once workers have been trained in new approaches to AOD problems, the process of change *has begun*, but it is far from complete. Changing assessments, ensuring that new forms are used and understood, establishing clear referral agreements with outside agencies—all these subsequent stages of AOD-CWS innovation have to happen *after* effective training has brought new forms of daily practice to line workers. A staff member in Louisville described the limited impact of training by saying, "I've been to a half-dozen trainings on AOD and they don't make any difference by themselves." Or, as one observer of the Sacramento reforms put it, "they loved the training, but they hated the implementation." Again, it was the external influence of the CPS crisis above all that led to the partial rejection of the new practice guidelines, not opposition to the concept of looking harder at AOD problems of parents in the CPS system.

---

managers who presumably rose to their positions because they had mastered their responsibilities. The assumption is not always warranted, but the resistance to training that follows from the assumption is often a problem.

 **"What should stay the same" in Sacramento's AODTI?** The question "What should stay the same?" is addressed in CWS reform when innovators take into account the time costs of new assessment forms. In Sacramento's CWS reform, an effort was made at one point to observe a guideline summarized as "no net increases in time." This means that if new assessment forms are required, some of the old forms should be dropped or consolidated. For the Sacramento AODTI, the answer to the question was the time that workers spend per case must stay the same, unless new resources are brought into the agency.

Lesson #7

Innovation requires results-based accountability to determine whether practice and policy are really changing.

Innovation without accountability becomes merely rhetorical talking about change. A "tight feedback loop" that monitors the changes expected from the organization will enable a quicker response to lagging implementation, but it demands that the information systems be in place to provide that feedback. If workers are expected to change their daily practice, their compliance must be monitored regularly enough to provide accountability. If community agencies are expected to become more active in working with noncrisis families, the extent to which this is happening must be monitored by intake information or some other form of useful feedback. "How will we know that the new process is happening?" is not yet an outcome question—but it is a critical question, because without compliance with the new procedures, the intended outcomes will never happen.

It is also important not to overload an innovation with new hardware and software that defeats its own purpose. Sometimes automation means that data are collected solely for the sake of collection, without being connected to monitoring either workers' compliance or client outcomes. A decent data system can catch noncompliance, but the trick is designing a system that isn't so cumbersome that it produces noncompliance.

Finally, it must be clear that if CWS-AOD reform seeks new accountability for results with clients, this inevitably brings new accountability for work performed by line workers and their operating units. Such accountability is unusual at the operating level of most CPS agencies, and within AOD systems as well. The impact of this new form of accountability should not be understated in negotiations with workers' representatives and with senior supervisors.

 In Sacramento County, the capacity of the new information system to monitor both the number of clients seen by AOD counselors and the number of assessments performed by CPS workers brought some strong reactions from both sets of workers, none of whom had been held accountable at that level in the past. But in both cases, for senior managers to have such information for the first time led to some important readjustments in caseloads and responsibilities that would have been impossible before the information system changes were made.

When innovation is accompanied by changes in the information systems that monitor workers' performance and client outcomes, the organization may for the first time be dealing with direct connections between what workers do and the results of what they do. This can be extremely unsettling. An innovation that is primarily oriented to training may be popular; adding assessment forms designed to track clients' needs and progress in treatment and determine if workers are changing their practice may be far less popular. Assessment forms can help diagnose and track clients; they also can detect *what workers are really doing differently.*

Lesson #8
In reforming systems, process and product need to be balanced.

Working across agencies that are unaccustomed to working together at all can sometimes make participants feel as if meetings alone actually represent progress. But they do not, and it is important to remember that they do not. To be sure, the process of building trust across AOD and CWS agencies is crucial, and that process takes time. But there must eventually be a product beyond the talking and trust building, or the process will have *become* the product—and no meeting in itself ever protected a child or supported a parent.

The good news is that state and local agencies and their nonprofit partners around the nation have increasingly used new tools for "putting the pieces together" across different service systems. These *policy tools* are capable of developing solid products that can lead a group of interagency or community-level partners beyond meetings and pilot projects to working at scale:

- Data-matching techniques for determining which clients are served by more than one agency or need resources from more than one agency.

- Case reviews that can accomplish the same purpose.

- Resource mapping and geocoding services information, using geographic information software that compiles information about informal community supports, formal public spending, and sites of services facilities or service incidents in a given neighborhood.

- Itemized "children's budgets" and budgets of total prevention spending in a community to documenting the costs of negative outcomes over time.

- Comprehensive inventories of substance abuse-related spending (such as Arizona's) to document and allocate by category all state AOD spending.

- Benchmarking to determine what outcomes and performance measures have been achieved by similar programs in other communities, using scorecards of neighborhood conditions and results-based accountability systems for program- and agency-focused outcomes.

- A collaborative values inventory (as described above) to assess a collaborative's willingness to address values issues that underlie policy choice, based on the degree of consensus within the group on those values.

- Collaborative matrices to identify all of the collaboration and coalitions that may be working on children and family issues in a given community.

- Evaluation of training content to determine whether the intended competencies are connected to the materials taught and the methods used.

Lesson #9

One size won't fit all.

The project prospectus for the Clark Foundation Community Partnerships makes this lesson explicit:

> The diversity of family behaviors that are represented in the abuse and neglect literature requires that communities' strategies respond to a wide range of family situations, and respond in an individualized fashion. "One size fits all" does not work to address this problem [Center for the Study of Social Policy 1997].

As the quote underscores, this need for diversity is true of responses to families and also of responses to communities. As a result, practitioners should be suspicious of any set of guidelines—including those in this work—that may purport to be "the only way to do it." There are definitely some broad principles that should be followed, and some powerful signals about how *not* to do it. But tailoring an innovation to local contexts is crucial to the innovation being fully rooted and accepted in that location, and to being sustained if it proves successful.

References

Calicchia, M., & Ginsburg, L. (1996). *Caring for our children: Labor's role in human services reform.* Washington, DC: AFL-CIO, Public Employee Department.

Center for the Study of Social Policy. (1997). *Strategies to keep children safe: Why community partnerships will make a difference.* Washington, D.C.: Author.

Christian, S. (1997). *New directions for child protective services.* Denver, CO: National Conference of State Legislatures.

Gardner, S. L. (Forthcoming). *Beyond collaboration to results.* Fullerton, CA: The Center for Collaboration for Children and Tempe, AZ: Arizona State University.

Schorr, L. (1997). *Common purpose: Strengthening families and neigh-borhoods to rebuild America.* New York: Doubleday.

Smale, G. G. (1996). *Mapping change and innovation.* London: National Institute for Social Work.

Weiner, M. (1982). *Human services management.* New York: The Dorsey Press.

4

Treating AOD Problems:
Practices, Innovations, and Effectiveness

The AOD field has begun to address the issues of children and families in treatment programs. Child welfare agencies and workers have not generally been familiar with these changes, however. Some observers familiar with both CWS and AOD systems believe that the AOD field has changed more than CWS in the areas where the two systems interact. Some of these changes were primarily due to the federal and state funding provided to AOD agencies for pregnant and parenting women's treatment programs, since the populations served by those programs overlap to some extent with the CWS population. But what has been missing is a needed connection between CWS and the mainstream of AOD treatment that goes beyond earmarked funding for categorical programs for some CWS clients.

The AOD treatment system is neither a black box of psychotherapies nor a monolithic entity admitting every client into a set treatment protocol involving "substitution" or "detox" medication. Recent developments in assessment and matching protocols have improved client-focused needs assessment and referral to appropriate services. The Center for Substance Abuse Treatment (CSAT) has recently published a report on the diverse strategies used in AOD treatment [CSAT 1997]. This chapter focuses on the most important AOD treatment innovations and suggests how these changes might help forge stronger links between CWS and AOD.

Comprehensive AOD Treatment and Disease Management

As described by the Director of the National Institute on Drug Abuse, comprehensive treatment is a mixture of pharmacological and behavioral therapy approaches that provide the tools for managing the chronic, relapsing disease of alcohol and drug dependence over the long term [Leshner 1994]. The time period that is emphasized in modern AOD approaches is a critical distinction; continuing disease management is stressed, not one-shot treatment. The disease management approach to drug dependence, in this sense, is similar to physicians managing patients with chronic conditions such as diabetes and hypertension, and is distinct from emergency services administered for acute illnesses.

One recent summary from the behavioral treatment field highlighted the following features of disease management:

- A treatment focus on a costly, chronic condition, disease, or diagnosis;

- A coordinated approach across multidisciplinary treatment teams;

- Use of evidence-based best practices proven to be highly effective;

- An education-intensive orientation that focuses on both patient and provider;

- An approach to care management that emphasizes both clinical efficacy and cost-effectiveness; and

- A method of systematic data collection that is clinically and financially evaluative [Vega 1998].

In contrast, CWS agencies often approach AOD problems from a "one-shot approach" rather than from a longer term disease management perspective. This plays out in practice in at least two critical ways: (1) instituting drug-testing programs, which are used as a measure of readiness to parent, with failed drug tests interpreted as clear markers of "failed" treatment; and (2) in expectations of treatment outcomes and clients' compliance with treatment protocols.

In the AOD treatment field, in contrast, positive drug urine tests are more commonly seen as an indication that a client requires more structure and intensity in the treatment program. State-of-the-art AOD treatment adjusts the intensity and structure provided to a client based on the client's progress and improved ability to exercise personal responsibility. These adjustments to program intensity are depicted in Table 3, which is adapted from a model developed by Dr. Vivian Brown, CEO of PROTOTYPES, and Dr. George Huber of The Measurement Group from evaluation documents of PROTOTYPES Women's Center in Pomona, California.* PROTOTYPES, Centers for Innovation in Health, Mental Health and Social Service programs include each of the levels of care so that they can respond to differing needs of women and their children.

The American Society of Addiction Medicine (ASAM) has developed patient placement criteria to assess which treatment options and levels of intensity are appropriate for clients [ASAM 1996]. Complete details, explanation, and training on implementing the criteria are available through ASAM.** This range of care allows some clients to participate in treatment services while they are also completing elements in their child welfare plan (e.g., parenting classes) or complying with job participation requirements under TANF. However, it is clear that clients who are more impaired require more intensive levels of care. In addition, clients who are not successful in a specific level of care generally require more intensive services and structure in their treatment plan. Unfortunately, CWS staff unfamiliar with the AOD system often see treatment as a bipolar set of extremes, involving either no-cost 12-step programs or expensive residential treatment.

Determination of the appropriate level of care is made by assessing a client's level of functioning in six life areas:

- Acute intoxication and/or withdrawal potential,

- Biomedical conditions,

---

* PROTOTYPES Women's Center, Dr. Vivian Brown, Executive Director. 5601 West Slauson Avenue, Suite 200, Culver City, CA 90230; 310/649-4347.
** The American Society of Addiction Medicine can be contacted at 4601 N. Park Avenue, Suite 101, Chevy Chase, MD 20815; 301/656-3920; e-mail: email@asam.org; URL: www.asam.org).

Table 3. Results of Adjusting Intensity and Severity of Treatment

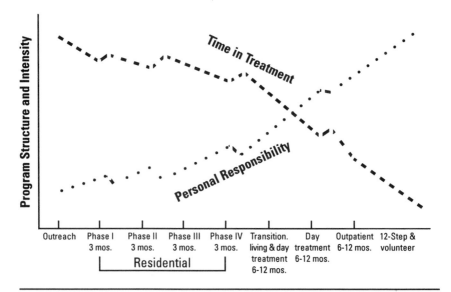

	Outreach	Phase I 3 mos.	Phase II 3 mos.	Phase III 3 mos.	Phase IV 3 mos.	Transition. living & day treatment 6-12 mos.	Day treatment 6-12 mos.	Outpatient 6-12 mos.	12-Step & volunteer

Residential (spanning Phase I through Phase IV)

- Emotional/behavioral conditions and complications,

- Treatment acceptance/resistance,

- Relapse/continued use potential, and

- Recovery environment (family and social situations).

The AOD field has reached some consensus in attempting to standardize treatment according to the levels-of-care distinction. In addition to detoxification services that can be delivered within each of the levels of care, ASAM PPC-2 criteria include three levels of outpatient care and four levels of residential care, as follows:

- Level 0.5 Early Intervention

- Level I Outpatient Services

    - I-D Ambulatory Detoxification without Extended On-site Monitoring

- I Outpatient Treatment

- Level II Intensive Outpatient/Partial Hospitalization Services

  - II-D Ambulatory Detoxification with Extended On-site Monitoring
  - II.1 Intensive Outpatient Treatment
  - II.5 Partial Hospitalization Treatment

- Level III Residential/Inpatient Services

  - III.1 Clinically Managed, Low-Intensity Residential Treatment (Halfway House; Supportive Living Environment)
  - III.2-D Clinically Managed Inpatient Detoxification Services (Social Detoxification)
  - III.3 Clinically Managed, Medium-Intensity Residential Treatment (Extended Residential Program)
  - III.5 Clinically Managed, Medium/High-Intensity Residential Treatment (Therapeutic Community)
  - III.7-D Medically Monitored Inpatient Detoxification Services
  - III.7 Medically Monitored Intensive Inpatient Treatment

- Level IV Medically Managed Intensive Inpatient Services

  - IV-D Medically Managed Inpatient Detoxification Services
  - IV Medically Managed Intensive Inpatient Treatment

Once in treatment, there are several approaches that are used. The specific therapeutic approaches are generally divided into three categories, with some adding a fourth: (1) physical methods, (2) psychological methods, (3) social methods, and (4) spiritual methods [Coles 1995; Mee-Lee 1995]. The categories are described in Table 4.

The CWS perception of AOD treatment as a one-shot approach affects what child welfare workers expect from their clients. CWS workers at times express their frustration that even when they are

Table 4. Therapeutic Approaches to AOD Treatment

Physical Methods	Psychological Methods	Social Methods	Spiritual Methods
Detoxification	Group, family, and individual	Legal strategies	Religiously oriented
Medications	psychotherapy	Rehabilitation	self-help groups
Acupuncture	Aversion therapy	Social skills training	
	Behavior modification	Self-help groups and	
		mutual aid	

able to make the linkage for AOD services for clients, they simply don't comply with treatment. In a recent meeting in a large county, that perception was expressed by an individual who represents children in juvenile dependency court actions. With unconscious irony, she stated, "We know all that research says that treatment is successful, but they just don't stay in treatment." Although multiple failed attempts to stop smoking (and resultant relapses) are readily accepted as common, the public is less willing to tolerate multiple attempts to stop the use of illicit drugs or the abuse of alcohol. We will return to this issue of treatment effectiveness below.

Treatment Innovations

Treatment Outcomes

Over the past decade, under considerable pressure from managed care in the behavioral health arena and other funders of AOD services, the AOD field has changed significantly, developing and implementing systems to evaluate treatment outcomes. Although states and local governments are at different stages of implementation, there has been an implicit consensus reached on the types of outcomes that are desired and measured among AOD agencies serving publicly funded clients. An important development has been the field's acceptance of outcomes in clients' daily functioning as measures of progress that go beyond total abstinence from AOD use. While abstinence is a desired goal, AOD agencies recognize that clients improve their level of functioning in multiple areas of daily living even before they reach abstinence. Obviously, millions of middle-income parents who are not abstinent are deemed adequate parents by society.

Treatment Is About Human Beings

For all the importance of treatment protocols, levels of care, and managed care coverages, it is sometimes possible to lose sight of the reality that treatment is about human beings. The connection between a counselor, a peer helper, an outreach worker, and a person trying to recover from addiction is a profound bond that rests as much on human relationships as on programmatic design. Every day, a good program draws the line between what treatment can do and what an AOD-dependent person must do for herself, and that choice is always mediated by a relationship of trust between two human beings. Assuring that workers in this field have the right training is critical, but assuring that they are good, resilient human beings is equally important, because what they are asked to do is to help individuals and families to change their lives, without any assurances that they will succeed. That these workers do succeed as often as they do is remarkable; that they keep trying to make a difference in the lives of other people is equally remarkable.

Ongoing efforts are identifying optimum measurement techniques and indicators of improved levels of functioning. Currently, the domains that are included in most client-level outcome systems are physical health, social and family relationships, mental health status, legal problems and criminal behavior, and employment/economic self-sufficiency. An important task for both the CWS and AOD fields is to clarify measures related to parenting competency, which have not generally been included in AOD outcomes research.

Managed Care

Although several states have implemented managed care approaches to financing AOD treatment, the vast majority of those states have only included the Medicaid portion of state and federal funding in those financing plans. However, many states and communities have implemented components of managed systems of care, such as matching clients to appropriate levels of care.

As previously discussed, AOD treatment varies in regard to the "intensity" of services delivered and in the degree of structured monitoring provided to the client [Young & Gardner 1997]. There are obvious cost differences between care in a highly structured setting and less intensive outpatient care. As noted in Chapter 1, this can further complicate the AOD-CWS connection, due to the role of managed care companies that can override treatment decisions made by AOD counselors and CWS workers. Authorizations for treatment, the level of care to be provided, and length of stay allowed in managed care settings may be determined by managed care staff who might be less familiar with the case and the special treatment needs of women involved with CWS.

Matching Services to Immediate Needs

A major component of early AOD treatment engagement is understanding the areas of life functioning that are being affected by the client's AOD use. The domains mentioned above are included in a biopsychosocial assessment and are linked to specific services in the treatment plan that address that domain. There is recent evidence that addressing the need that the client perceives as most urgent results in more effective client engagement in the treatment process and leads to better outcomes. The parallel in CWS, of course, is the family preservation worker who engages with a new family by asking what the family perceives as its most important needs, as opposed to simply starting weekly counseling sessions on parenting.

The innovation in AOD services is that, regardless of the level of care that the client is in (residential or outpatient), a comprehensive assessment enables the AOD worker to focus on the area of life that the client perceives as most urgent. Substance-abusing clients come to treatment with a host of interpersonal, legal, medical, financial, and other concerns. Making the connection between the immediate crisis that the client is experiencing and his/her substance use ensures that treatment addresses the reality of the client's related problems, rather than providing treatment in a vacuum that ignores those other issues.

Medications Development

Neurobiology and recent advances in biomedical research technology have developed new knowledge about molecular and cellular mechanisms involved in the disease of AOD abuse. For example, the ability to conduct noninvasive brain imaging has made it possible to study the effect of AOD abuse on the brain to literally "see a brain on drugs." Drug abuse researchers have identified and genetically specified the molecular brain receptors of all major abused drugs. These discoveries are leading to new medications that block the chemical actions of abused substances. At present, medications are available for use with opiate-dependent clients. Methadone has been used effectively since the early 1970s; LAAM (l-alpha-acetylmethadol) was made available in 1993. Naltrexone was approved in 1984 and is also being used in the treatment of alcoholism. Buprenorphine is in the clinical trail stage of development for opiate addiction. The development of medications for cocaine, however, is in its infancy.

Motivational Interviewing

Recent advances in AOD treatment research have repeatedly shown that persons who are coerced to participate in AOD treatment have similar outcomes as those who voluntarily participate in treatment. In fact, some treatment providers have specialized in conducting "interventions" with persons who are not yet able or willing to admit that their AOD use is the cause of substantial family, work, and health-related problems. Intervening with a person who has not yet admitted that he/she is "powerless" over alcohol and other drugs is a primary component of early treatment protocols and allows the individual to move past denial to a willingness to change.

This early work by treatment professionals is sometimes referred to as "raising the bottom," (i.e., not waiting until the client "hits bottom") so that the individual and society do not have to incur the higher costs of continued drug dependence. Ultimately, individual motivation is an important ingredient in recovery, but motivation can be greatly enhanced by AOD professionals providing cognitive, supportive, and behavioral interventions during early stages of recovery.

Much of the understanding of these early phases of treatment is based on work by Prochaska and DiClemente [1985], who proposed that change is a process rather than a discrete event. The change process has been described in phases with distinct goals for working with a client at each phase, as shown in Table 5 [Bell & Rollnick 1996].

Contingency Contracting

The vast majority of clients entering AOD treatment do so with an implicit contingency contract: for example, in response to a spouse's ultimatum ("go to treatment or get a divorce"); as a condition for regaining a driver's license; in order to keep a job; or as the result of "a nudge from the judge," the phrase used by many people in recovery to indicate how they got to mandated treatment. Contingency contracting relies on these and other motivations for a person to seek treatment, promote desired behaviors, and sanction undesired behavior. Critical components of contingency contracting are that the contingencies must be mutually agreed on, carefully monitored, consistently applied, and involve the significant others and institutions connected to the individual [Morgan 1996]. In CWS, this corresponds to the general idea of "differential sanctions," in which clients are rewarded or sanctioned as they progress in compliance with CWS requirements and the severity of their behavior.

The Philosophy and Continuum of Harm Reduction

Although harm reduction is often a lightning rod for debate about legalization of illicit drugs, the basic operating principle of harm reduction is that any positive change in AOD use helps. Harm reduction (HR) draws a distinction between intervention models requiring total abstinence as a prerequisite for access to treatment and those that focus on incremental improvements in lifestyle, which will ideally lead to abstinence and improved parental functioning. Harm reduction strategies seek to reduce the risks associated with AOD abuse and can achieve immediate improvement in individual and family functioning. The goal is to equip substance users to reduce the harm caused by their use to themselves, their families, and their community. Specific targets of HR strategies include improving the user's health sta-

Table 5. Phases in the Change Process

Phase	Aim of Intervention
Precontemplation	To increase the perception of risks associated with substance use by providing information and feedback
Contemplation	Explore the positive and negative consequences of use and tip the balance toward change
Determination	Preparation for change by strengthening the commitment to change by helping the client to determine the best course of action to take
Action	Acknowledge that the client may experience a sense of ambivalence and need a sense of reward for any success achieved
Maintenance	Requires continued vigilance toward the change process and achievement of personal goals
Relapse	Although not desirable, is a normal part of the change process and interventions are geared to minimizing problems associated with lapse or relapse by renewing the commitment to change

tus and reducing family violence, criminal behavior, poor parenting practices, and neglect or inattention to children's needs. Most HR strategies accept abstinence as the appropriate end goal but believe that even for those clients for whom abstinence is not achievable, major changes in life functioning are possible.

Harm reduction strategies are based on a public health approach to AOD problems and include such practices as strict laws against driving while intoxicated, designated drivers, and nicotine replacement patches and gum. For the illegal drugs, harm reduction strategies include decreasing the spread of HIV through needle-bleaching programs, Arizona's example of releasing nonviolent drug offenders with court jurisdiction over treatment compliance, agencies devising a "safety plan" for children with appropriate child care if parents are planning to use alcohol or other drugs, determining if the client's patterns of use could be altered to reduce associated harm, and determining if the method of drug use can be changed to a less harmful method.

Several reviewers of this guidebook commented that harm reduction strategies may be a part of the common ground that could be expanded as the conceptual bridge between AOD and CWS. From the CWS side, the overwhelming concern for child safety means that reducing potential harm to children is part of the basic mission of the agency. Therefore, a CWS/AOD dialogue about harm reduction can focus on the central issue of reducing harm to children while considering the behavior of parents in treatment and in recovery.

Treatment Effectiveness

Despite 25 years of research documenting treatment effectiveness[*] and cost offsets derived from AOD treatment [Langenbucher 1994], the perception persists among the public and many policymakers that treatment "doesn't work." Thus, it is necessary to deal with that skepticism in any discussion about expanding treatment services and linking them to the needs of parents in the CWS system.

Effectiveness of Treatment Among the General Population

At the macro level, several recent national- and state-level studies have documented outcomes derived from AOD treatment and have found rates of AOD recovery similar to those of other diseases that require a behavioral change component as part of the treatment regimen. In addition, research conducted by McLellan and his colleagues documented that AOD treatment compliance is comparable to compliance rates among patients treated for diabetes and hypertension, two other chronic diseases requiring major behavioral changes. Less than one-half of diabetics comply with their medication protocols and fewer than 30% of persons with high blood pressure comply with the medication and prescribed diets [McLellan et al. 1995].

CSAT released its National Treatment Improvement Evaluation Study (NTIES) in 1997. The study included more than 4,400 clients

---

[*] Two national studies prior to DATOS (described in this report) were the Drug Abuse Reporting program (DARP), which included treatment admissions between 1969 and 1973, and the Treatment Outcome Prospective Study (TOPS), which studied admissions between 1979 and 1981. DATOS included treatment admissions between 1991 and 1993.

in the outcome analysis from 78 treatment centers across the country. Looking for changes in behavior from before treatment to after treatment, they found that drug use was cut by half, criminal behavior was reduced up to 80%, employment significantly increased, homelessness decreased, and there were significant improvements in physical and mental health leading to reductions in medical costs [SAMHSA 1997].

The National Institute on Drug Abuse in 1997 released findings from the Drug Abuse Treatment Outcome Study (DATOS), which tracked 10,000 drug abusers from almost 100 treatment programs who entered treatment between 1991 and 1993 in 11 cities. This is the third national outcome study since 1969. DATOS also used a before-to-after protocol and included four treatment types (outpatient methadone, long-term residential, outpatient drug-free, and short-term inpatient programs). DATOS found that drug use dropped significantly and that there were significant reductions in illegal acts and suicidal thoughts/attempts, while employment increased [Meuller & Wyman 1997]. Research has clearly demonstrated that among clients who are "harder to serve," those who receive "more support services in addition to basic drug abuse treatment were more likely to be abstinent at one-year follow-up than those who received fewer support services" [Anglin et al. 1997].

In addition, several state-level studies have documented the cost offsets that are derived from improving clients' functioning and the resultant decrease in societal costs resulting from AOD treatment.* Specifically, California found that $7 is saved for $1 investment in treatment [Gerstein 1994]; Oregon found that $5.60 in criminal justice, public assistance, health care, and victim and theft losses were avoided for every $1 spent on AOD treatment [Finigan 1996].

Remarkably, however, most analyses of the cost offsets of treatment done in the AOD system have excluded foster care from the

---

* See two compilations of state-level data on treatment effectiveness: Young, N. K. (1994). *Invest in treatment for alcohol and other drug problems: It pays* and Young, N. K. (1996). *Alcohol and other drug treatment: Policy choices in welfare reform.* Both are published and available from the National Association of State Alcohol and Drug Abuse Directors, Washington, DC; 202/293-0090.

calculations of treatment savings. Since much of the AOD research originated with prison populations, researchers have been more focused on cost offsets in the criminal justice, health, and employment systems. This exclusion has also been true of some of the studies assessing programs for pregnant and parenting women. One researcher admitted in a discussion with a federal official a few years ago, "We never thought to add data about foster care in the research design." This is another indicator of the distance between the two systems; it is difficult to document what an evaluation *doesn't* look for in its evaluation of outcomes.

Effectiveness of Treatment Among Women and Their Children

Many examples of successful women-oriented treatment programs have been documented by recent evaluation research. In 1995, the Center for Substance Abuse Treatment (CSAT) published findings from a study of its grantees that were administered by its Women and Children's Branch [CSAT 1995]. They found the following:

- Of women in treatment ...

    - 95% reported uncomplicated, drug-free births;
    - 81% who were referred by the criminal justice system have no new charges following their treatment;
    - 75% who successfully completed treatment remained drug free;
    - 46% obtained employment following treatment; and
    - 40% eliminated or reduced their dependence on welfare.

- Of their children ...

    - 65% were returned from foster care, and
    - 84% who participated in treatment with their mothers improved their school performance.

Each of the women's specialized treatment programs developed under CSAT funding has documented significant gains among the women and children enrolled. The majority of these programs have developed multidisciplinary approaches to meet the multiple needs of women and their children. The two programs highlighted here have developed linkages with a comprehensive network of providers and have documented outcomes in multiple domains. For example, PRO-TOTYPES Women's Center in Pomona, California, serves 80 women and 50 children at any one time in its residential treatment program. Follow-up research conducted by The Measurement Group* of 124 women six months after they departed from the PROTOTYPES residential program, compared outcomes for women who were in the program less than 180 days (short stay) with those who were in the program 180 days or longer (long stay). The evaluation found important differences among women who stayed in treatment more than six months as shown in Table 6.

These outcomes remain fairly consistent in the longer term as evidenced by Gateway Community Services in Jacksonville, Florida.** Almost 430 children were served in a three-year period of the residential and outpatient treatment program; 945 children did not reside with their mother when she was admitted to the residential program; 364 were reunified. There were 131 women who were pregnant at the time of admission, 130 babies were born drug free (one woman delivered a baby with a positive toxicology screen the same week she was admitted to treatment). The 364 children who were reunified with their mothers were given the Learning Accomplishment Profile when they were reunified with their mothers and after one year of participating in the extensive therapeutic services provided by the program. The developmental lag that can exist between drug-exposed children and their peers (in this sample, it was primarily in language and cognitive areas) had virtually disappeared by the second assessment point. Just over one-quarter of women admitted to Gateway's specialized programs were referred by the Department of Children and Families, as shown in Table 7. The predominant drug used by the women was cocaine, as shown in Table 8.

---

* The Measurement Group, Dr. George Huba. 5811 A Upland, Culver City, CA 90230.
** Gateway Community Services, Dr. Virginia Borrok, President/CEO. 555 Stockton Street, Jacksonville, FL 32204; 904/387-4661.

Table 6. Comparison of Length of Stay in Treatment

Outcome Domain	Short Stay < 180 days	Long Stay > 180 days	Total Sample
AOD Abstinence	70%	94%	85%
Employment	48%	63%	57%
No New Arrests	72%	96%	87%
Homelessness	9%	4%	6%

Table 7. Sources of Referral

| Referral Source | Percentage of Admissions | | |
	Residential	Outpatient	Total
Department of Children and Families	11%	52%	28%
Other AOD Provider	24%	20%	22%
Legal System	34%	4%	21%
Voluntary	26%	2%	16%
Hospital	5%	9%	8%
Public Health	2%	12%	6%

Table 8. Drugs Used by Women in Study

| Primary Drug Used At Admission | Percentage of Women | |
	Residential Program	Outpatient Program
Cocaine	44%	70%
Cocaine and other drugs	47%	19%
Alcohol	7%	7%
Prescription abuse	1%	1%
Marijuana	1%	3%

Among women served by Gateway's Women's Recovery Program, the overall treatment completion rate is comparable to many other AOD treatment agencies. Among women admitted to residential treatment, 46% completed treatment, and among women admitted to intensive outpatient services, 49% completed treatment. To evaluate the program, a random sample of 60 women was followed for four years (30 women were discharged from the residential program and

30 from intensive outpatient services). At one year after their treatment discharge:

- 72% of the women reported being clean from alcohol and other drugs;

- 64% attained education and/or vocational skills necessary for employment;

- 52% were employed one year after discharge; and

- 92% reported no further involvement with police, court, or probation one year after discharge.

A network of community-based programs serving women and their children in New York City has recently documented AOD treatment outcomes that were reported by Magura and his colleagues from the National Development and Research Institutes and the New York City Administration for Children's Services [Magura et al. 1998]. Women who had given birth to a drug-exposed infant were given priority for treatment admission; women with children less than 6 years old were also eligible for the program. Families received home-based casework, social services, and substance abuse treatment. The program used public contracts with community-based and culturally sensitive family service agencies and outpatient substance abuse treatment. The program goals were to prevent foster care placement and to provide adequately for the family's needs.

The evaluators followed 173 mothers for an average of 30 months after their admission to treatment. Similar to Gateway's data described above, 49% of women exited treatment before completion. There were 13% who transferred to other programs; 28% had completed treatment at the follow-up point and 9% were still in treatment. Projecting from the 49% who exited treatment to the 9% who were still in treatment gave a projected overall completion rate of 33% of the 173 treatment admissions.

In the overall group, there were no significant reductions between admission and one-year follow-up in the percentage of parents with

---

Funders and Effectiveness

It is also important to recognize that some public agencies in both CWS and AOD fields have not done all that they could to use their own authority to address the issue of the effectiveness of treatment. When a public child welfare agency is critical of the effectiveness of treatment, but has done little to document the actual experience of their own clients as they go in and out of treatment, it makes it harder to change the treatment system. Similarly, in some consolidated agencies with responsibility for both AOD and CWS issues, when an agency is at the same time funding AOD treatment providers and criticizing the effectiveness of AOD treatment for its CWS clients, it does raise the question of why the providers are still funded and why contract oversight is not being used to leverage better outcomes or change providers.

---

children in out-of-home care. However, parents who completed or were still participating in treatment were significantly less likely to have children in foster care (16%) than parents who left treatment or were transferred (30%). Parents who completed or were still in treatment were also significantly less likely to have children living elsewhere at follow-up (20%) compared to parents who left treatment or were transferred (48%).

Important distinctions were apparent, however, among parents who did not have children in foster care when they were admitted to treatment. Only 6% of parents who completed or were still active in treatment had children placed in foster care between admission and follow up. But 23% of parents who left or transferred had some children placed in foster care at follow-up. There were too few parents who had children in foster care at admission to evaluate reunification rates.

Producing these results is much less costly than jail, prison, or foster care costs. For example, the publicly funded reimbursement rates in California for the treatment continuum at PROTOTYPES ranges in reimbursement levels from $41.16 for a MediCal-reimbursed group session (in California, Medicaid is called MediCal and covers drug treatment for a woman while she is pregnant and 60 days after the birth of her baby), to intensive outpatient care that is reimbursed at the rate of $72.75 per day, and on to the residential therapeutic community at a rate of $85 per day for a woman and her child. The additional costs of treatment are paid by private grants and fundraising activities.

Prior to implementation of training in Sacramento County, there were 11 AOD treatment groups conducted by AOD counselors. After participating in the Level III training, social workers, nurses, and AOD counselors instituted 24 additional groups. The different types of groups included AOD information and education, pretreatment groups for clients waiting for space at a community provider, and AOD intervention and supports.

A total of 165 parents who were assessed for AOD problems were randomly selected from the CWS caseload for follow-up. The 165 parents had 530 children; at the first assessment point, 247 children were living with their parent. Of the 165 parents, 50 graduated from group treatment, 39 dropped out, 37 were assessed with an AOD problem but never attended a group, and 39 were assessed as "no AOD problem" and were selected as a comparison. The chart on page 96 highlights the improvements in children's custody status among group treatment graduates and the decline in the percentage of children living with their parents among those parents assessed with AOD problems who did not participate in the group services. The percentage change is calculated between the time that their parents were assessed for AOD problems and at three-months postassessment. (One-year follow-up data are currently being collected.)

Despite these findings of treatment effectiveness and cost savings, CWS workers often tell us that what they need in dealing with specific families in their caseloads is help from AOD agencies in making earlier decisions about moving children to more stable homes when parents are not successful in treatment, as is increasingly required in concurrent planning. This is an area for which the AOD field must take responsibility. AOD practitioners could offer much assistance to CWS in

Parents' Status	Children's Living Arrangement - Number (and Percent)					
	At Assessment		At 3-month Follow-up		Percentage Change from Assessment to 3-month Follow-up	
	Living w/ parent	Not w/ parent	Living w/ parent	Not w/ parent	Living w/ parent	Not w/ parent
Graduated	61 (25%)	91 (37%)	76 (37%)	79 (26%)	+48%	-30%
Dropped out	64 (25%)	75 (31%)	44 (21%)	104 (34%)	+15%	+10%
Never attended	51 (26%)	36 (15%)	32 (16%)	62 (21%)	-24%	+33%
No AOD problem	71 (28%)	42 (17%)	53 (26%)	58 (19%)	-7%	+12%
Total	247 (100%)	244 (100%)	205 (100%)	303(100%)	--	--

helping to determine early signs of "readiness to change." However, CWS workers must also take responsibility to understand AOD treatment and to work with AOD professionals in determining when AOD-abusing parents are able to protect and nurture their children.

To move away from a one-shot treatment and toward a disease management approach, *CWS will need to move beyond a one-size-fits-all approach to AOD problems with the knowledge that one method and one set of rules will not work for all clients.* However, there are commonalities among programs that have documented treatment effectiveness. Key ingredients in effective drug treatment programs have been delineated by Waltman:

- Easy accessibility,

- Treatment flexibility,

- Involvement of other family members,

- Matching treatment to salient client variables,

- Good therapists,

- Motivated clients,

- Client accountability for their sobriety,

- Focused treatment approaches,

- Follow-up of dropouts and program graduates, and

- Aftercare supportive services [Waltman 1995].

In addition, client characteristics associated with better outcomes have been identified. Of particular importance are employment, social/family support, and having a mental health diagnosis in addition to the substance abuse. In a recent review of treatment outcomes, 11 factors were identified as critical variables and are listed in Table 9 [Alemi et al. 1995]. Two things are clear: (1) women involved with the child welfare and welfare systems in many cases will fall into the harder-to-serve group, and (2) these clients will therefore need more intensive services, and in some cases, more time to succeed in moving to work. For CWS clients, as discussed above, the time required may conflict with the timetables for termination of parental rights, TANF limits, or the needs of the child.

Enhancing Effectiveness: The Special Needs of Women

In working with the child welfare and general welfare populations, special consideration should be made for the treatment needs of women. Reviews of the literature on women's treatment issues often mention the following critical components of women's AOD treatment programs:

- Many women seeking treatment for AOD problems have been victims of physical and/or sexual abuse; these complex issues can often be triggers for relapse and most often need to be addressed in gender-specific programs by women treatment professionals. The term "women with multiple vulnerabilities" refers to women who enter AOD treatment with co-occurring mental health disorders, HIV risk and/or disease, and trauma (either family violence or sexual assault histories).

Table 9. Critical Variables Affecting Treatment Outcomes

Domain	Client Barriers to Success	Client Strengths and Assets
Age	Under age 30	Over age 30
Employment	Unemployed with little work history	Stable employment history
Motivation	Little acceptance of AOD problems	Desire to recover
Consequences and sanctions	Little fear of AOD-related consequences (e.g., loss of job or custody of children)	Fear of consequences reinforced by sanctions
Physical and social environment	Return to a neighborhood where drugs are readily available and with a drug-using peer group	Little contact with a "drug culture" and fewer life stressors (e.g., poverty)
Legal status and peer criminality	Numerous pretreatment arrests and a peer group involved with criminal acts	Few pretreatment arrests and a noncriminally involved peer group
Social Support	Family members or peers who cause interpersonal conflicts or fail to support goals of recovery	Family members and peer who exert pressure to stop substance use and provide emotional support for recovery
History of drug use	Using a variety of drugs, frequent drug use, younger age at onset of addiction, a longer course of addiction, and few days of sobriety prior to entering treatment	Use of a primary substance, older onset of addiction, a period of abstinence prior to treatment admissions
History of treatment	Numerous treatment attempts	Longer length of time in treatment
Dual diagnosis and psychological problems	Significant psychiatric problems, high levels of anger, depression, childhood sexual abuse	No concurrent psychiatric disorders
Chronic illness	Significant chronic illnesses (e.g., arthritis, back pain, asthma, emphysema, ulcers)	Good physical health

- The three greatest barriers to women seeking and remaining in treatment are stigma, fear of losing custody of their children, and the lack of child care for their children while they are in treatment.

- Specialized services for women should include health and nutrition, intervention for family and community violence, intervention for children who may be affected by prenatal drug exposure, housing needs, parenting education and skill building, vocational training, and employment assistance [DHHS 1995]. In addition, many women's providers have added literacy training, therapeutic recreation, and vocational skill building. A family focus in designing and implementing these programs is critical.

- Additional components that are specifically added for the population of parents in treatment who are involved with the child welfare system include shared family care and the use of volunteers and kinship care to support parents in treatment [Barth 1994].

AOD treatment providers have responded to these special needs of women and have developed programs that either deliver these multiple services on site or in coordination with other service providers.

The Need for Targeted Intervention and Prevention for Children "in the System"

More comprehensive assessment and targeted intervention is needed for all children, youth, and families who overlap the child welfare and juvenile justice systems. Although attention to prenatally exposed infants is critical and renewed efforts have focused attention on services for adolescents, interventions for younger children (ages 5 to 12) of substance-abusing parents are still scarce, and these "middle children" are at high risk of developing their own AOD problems. This section reviews the needs of all three of these age groups of children.

The needs of children of alcoholics (COAs) and children of substance abusers (COSAs) can be viewed in a developmental approach. It is well established that infants and young children have specific needs for adequate bonding and attachment with their caregivers. In recent years, we have gained new insights into the critical early years for brain development in young children. These early years for children with substance-abusing parents become critical years for intervention to assure that children receive appropriate stimulation, opportunities for brain development, and emotional well-being through bonding and attachment for infants and younger children.

We are continuing to miss the large group of children between early childhood and adolescence who need AOD interventions. These children—neither adolescents nor in the 2 to 5 percent of CWS children who were identified as prenatally exposed—should be a critical subset served by any expansion of AOD treatment services for children.

> ### Look for the Other Children in the Family
> In assessing prevalence, it is extremely important for child welfare agencies to assume that AOD is a family disease and *to look for involved siblings*. Recent work by Richard Barth and Barbara Needell of the Child Welfare Research Center at the University of California at Berkeley concluded that abandoned and neglected infants brought into foster care in 1995 had siblings in foster care in a ratio of 1.7 siblings for every infant in foster care. Barth and Needell conclude, "Clearly, a few parents who continue to generate births of children born exposed to substances have a substantial impact on the foster care caseload."

The childhood years also require opportunities to develop self-concept and self-esteem that are cultivated through curiosity, initiative, and independence. For COAs and COSAs, these opportunities are often disrupted, which interferes with normal development. These children need services that specifically address their families' AOD problems, including group interventions with their peers and formal treatment. They also need supportive adults to reinforce the message that their parents' AOD abuse is not their fault and is not the path their own life needs to take. The Children of Alcoholics Foundation states that support groups for school-age children help to build resiliency and protective factors in the following ways [Richardson & Weinstein 1997]:

- Bolstering self-esteem,

- Providing support,

- Providing consistency,

- Teaching coping skills,

- Encouraging adaptive distancing,

- Providing a positive adult role model, and

- Encouraging mutual aid.

The National Association for Children of Alcoholics has developed an excellent set of core competencies needed by health care providers in caring for children and adolescents in families affected by substance abuse [NACA 1997]. They suggest three levels of competencies based on the levels of responsibility that the health care provider takes for the care of children. Needed competencies range from awareness and communication skills in Level I, to assessment and care management in Level II, to medical and behavioral treatment in Level III.*

For youth who become chemically dependent, a developmental perspective and approach to treatment is imperative. Most AOD treatment programs were originally developed for adult males. Just as the AOD field has adapted to a growing need for treatment services that are responsive to the unique needs of women, the AOD field must also be responsive to the unique needs of adolescents. The Berkshire Farm Center and Services for Youth in New York has developed treatment programs based on a clear delineation of the differences between adult and youth AOD treatment.** Bob Kirkman and Bill Hill of Berkshire Farm contributed the following section on youth-oriented treatment.

Recent advances in AOD treatment have shown that programs for youth must include the characteristics, maturational effects, and developmental processes of adolescents into their program design and delivery. The critical differences between youth and adults' AOD-related problems and treatment include the following:

- *Rapid progression.* Adolescents often make the progression from first use to full chemical dependence within a period of 6 to 18 months; among adults, a two- to seven-year period is common to develop a chemical use disorder.

---

* National Association for Children of Alcoholics, Sis Wenger, Executive Director. 11426 Rockville Pike, Suite 100, Rockville, MD 20852; 301/468-0985.
** Berkshire Farm Center and Services for Youth. 13640 Route 33, Canaan, New York 12029; 518/781-4567.

- *Narrow repertoire of coping skills.* Unlike adults, who often arrive at the chemically dependent stage with an array of coping strategies developed by life experiences, adolescent chemical dependence is such that the development of these strategies is curtailed at the stage in which they began using alcohol, tobacco, and other drugs. For this reason, treatment of adolescent chemical dependence requires habilitation focus and requires more comprehensive treatment intervention than adult rehabilitation models.

- *Stronger denial system.* Adolescents experience a stronger system of denial because, unlike adult addicts/alcoholics, they typically have not experienced the years of negative consequences related to their AOD use that adults have. As a result, they tend to have more difficulty connecting their problems to their drug use.

- *Stronger enabling system.* There is a wider acceptance of drug use by the adolescent peer group and this greater acceptance supports and normalizes drug taking and drug-related behavior.

- *Maturational delays.* Adolescents experience cognitive, affective, and behavioral/maturational delays directly caused by drug use. The younger that drug use is initiated, the greater the delays experienced in the maturation process.

- *Developmental issues.* Chemical dependence impacts negatively on the adolescent developmental tasks of individuation, separation, and autonomy. These are necessary developmental processes for transitions to young adulthood.

Given these characteristics and developmental processes, adolescents tend to be less willing and able to adapt to "abstinence only" programs in comparison to adults. Berkshire Farms has found that their adolescent programs need to embrace a motivational approach that reinforces the continuum from harm reduction to abstinence. Their program model is depicted in Table 10.

Review: Implications of AOD Treatment Innovation for CWS

Throughout this discussion of AOD treatment, the child welfare implications have been evident:

- The need to deal with the skepticism, lack of information, and different time frames of the CWS worker;

- The importance of operating on the assumption that children who are the focus of a CPS complaint and their siblings are affected directly by their parents' AOD abuse and may need intervention or treatment themselves;

- The need to consider the developmental stages of children from infancy through adolescence in assessing the impacts of parental substance abuse and the need for treatment for the children as well;

- The need to understand what AOD treatment can and cannot accomplish; and

- The importance of balancing both realistic expectations and solid information about different forms of AOD treatment as they support women and their children in moving toward the goal of a stable family.

Child welfare agencies do not need to be, nor should they try to become, experts in AOD treatment. They need to know enough about their own clients, however, to interact with the AOD system in more depth than merely handing a client a list of phone numbers of treatment centers or assuming that clients with substance abuse problems will never be able to gain control of their lives. The AOD field has the burden of communicating its successes and methods more clearly with

Table 10. Adolescent Program Model

		Engagement along the Continuum of Treatment
H **A** **R** **M**	*Motivation Phase*	• Development of a framework to evaluate whether a problem exists in major life areas • Identification of goals • Identification of problems • Identificationand development of strategies and techniques to meet goals and to overcome barriers to goal attainment • Development of a *Community Safety Plan*

R **E** **D** **U** **C** **T** **I** **O** **N** **TO** **A** **B** **S**	*Stabilization Phase*	• Client establishes a personal focus of treatment
		• Development of a problem management plan emphasizing:
		  1. Feeling management
		  2. Urge management strategies
		  3. Behavior and situational management strategies
		• Development of a *Community Problem Management Plan*

T **I** **N** **E** **N** **C** **E**	*Early Recovery Phase*	• Formal relapse prevention planning • Recovery-based lifestyle planning • Development of a *Community Recovery Plan*

child welfare agencies with whom they share clients; the CWS field has the burden of listening and linking this new information into their efforts to preserve families and keep children safe and nurtured.

Summary: Treatment Effectiveness and the CWS Client

As noted in this section, several studies of women's treatment programs cluster their findings around the figure of one-third of parents, typically mothers, who successfully complete treatment on their first admission to a program. Other data and lengthy discussion with sev-

AOD Treatment Pays, Even When It Succeeds
for Only Some Parents

Due to the high cost of out-of-home care, if treatment succeeds and families are reunified for only one-third of the parents referred from the CWS system, the costs that are avoided far exceed the total costs of AOD treatment. So treatment does not need to succeed for all clients to produce a net positive result.

A hypothetical scenario. One hundred women are treated at the highest average treatment cost ($6,800 per client in residential care in the NTIES study), for a total of $680,000. They average 1.5 children each for a total of 150 children.

If children average seven years in out-of-home care, at a low estimate of $6,000 per year, the total foster care cost is $42,000 per child. If 30 parents reunify with 45 children (which is a conservative success rate), the foster care costs avoided by those 45 are $1,890,000, repaying the total treatment cost for the original 100 women three times over.

When the other offsets from AOD treatment and avoided out-of-home care (e.g., reduced health care, criminal justice, and welfare costs) are added in, the ratio improves even more substantially, even if it is assumed that some public costs are still borne once the children are reunified.* The benefits increase further if an assumption is made that some portion of the parents are not successful on their first treatment episode but continue with subsequent readmissions and succeed, as evidence strongly suggests.

---

* Assumptions of Treatment Costs and Benefits for CWS Clients: (1) It is assumed that parents who are referred for AOD treatment are from the more serious portion of the CPS caseload, with a greater likelihood of having their parental rights terminated. (2) It is assumed that the average episode in foster care, which is 12 months for *all* children, is much longer for children with AOD-abusing parents. An estimate of 7 years has been derived from experience in Los Angeles County and is used in these figures. (3) It is assumed that once these children are reunified, half will require Medicaid and other public subsidies for 4 years at an average cost of $5,000 per child beyond foster care costs, or a total cost of $450,000. It is further assumed that the other half will require no public subsidy, saving $787,500 more in nonfoster care costs. Thus the net savings in nonfoster care costs is $337,500.

eral exemplary providers suggest that the percentage improves to one-third of the remainder, or 22% of the total, who become successful completers after multiple attempts. The evidence is strong that the more readmissions, the more likely will be eventual successful completion. Thus, a total of slightly more than one-half of the admissions to a given program can be assumed to become successful completers—some after one episode of treatment admission, the others after multiple admissions to a program.

Clearly, if the developmental "clock" and the new federal requirements for time limits in both welfare and child welfare services are taken into account, some of these "successful" completers will still have lost their rights to be primary caretakers of their children by the time they are successful in treatment. But it also signals clearly that treatment for a significant segment of parents—though definitely not all—has the potential to reunite many of these parents with their children in a more stable family. That is the first and primary child welfare outcome against which AOD treatment is fairly measured.

But there is a second outcome as well: for those parents for whom the clock ran out before they successfully completed a program, it also says that these birth parents can continue as active, positive participants in the lives of their children, even though they are not serving as primary caretakers. That outcome must be contrasted with the "disappearing parent" who is so common in child welfare cases, resulting in serious negative effects on children in later life. The significance of reconnecting birth parents and children is also important in the context of kinship care, where relatives may make the reconnection process easier.

The importance of this is that it becomes a more refined position for advocates of closer AOD-CWS ties than claiming that all CWS families will benefit from AOD treatment. All CWS families with AOD problems *should be offered treatment appropriate to their needs*— and they should be compelled to at least enter treatment. But not all will complete it successfully after one or even repeated admissions. The realities of treatment include failure with some clients and success with others—sometimes with clients who may have seemed hopeless but who persevere throughout many obstacles, supported by professionals, peers, friends, and kin and driven by a deep desire to be reunited with their children.

The real achievements of treatment should not be discounted, but neither should the claim be made that treatment works for most clients in a single treatment episode. A balanced explanation of the effects of treatment on families should be part of the public education and social marketing of treatment. The point is that treatment does work for a significant group of clients *over time*, in ways that assure that treatment pays off and brings genuine improvement in the lives of children and families.

References

Alemi, F., Stephens, R. C., Llorens, S., & Orris, B. (1995). A review of factors affecting treatment outcomes: Expected treatment outcomes scale. *The American Journal of Drug and Alcohol Abuse*, 21 (4), 483-509.

American Society of Addiction Medicine. (1996). *Patient placement criteria for the treatment of substance-related disorders* (2nd ed.). Chevy Chase, MD: Author.

Anglin, M. D., Hser, Y., & Grella, C.E. (1997). Treatment histories: The long view of addiction. *NIDA Notes*, 12(5), 8.

Barth, R. P. (1994). Long-term in-home services. In D. Besharov (Ed.), *When drug addicts have children*. Washington, DC: Child Welfare League of America.

Bell, A., & Rollnick, A. (1996). Motivational interviewing in practice: A structured approach. In F. Rotners, D.S. Keller, & J. Morgenstern (Eds.). *Treating substance abuse: Theory and technique*. New York: The Guilford Press.

Center for Substance Abuse Treatment [CSAT]. (1997). *50 strategies for substance abuse treatment*. Rockville, MD: Author. May be ordered through the National Clearinghouse for Alcohol and Drug Information at 800/729-6686 or electronically at http://www.samhsa.gov.

Center for Substance Abuse Treatment [CSAT]. (1995). *Producing results*. Rockville, MD: Author.

Coles, C. D. (1995). Addiction and recovery: Impact of substance abuse on families. In G. H. Smith, C. D. Coles, M. K. Poulsen, & C. K. Cole (Eds.), *Children, families, and substance abuse: Challenges for changing educational and social outcomes* (pp. 40-44). Baltimore, MD: Paul H. Brookes Publishing Co.

Finigan, M. (1996). *Societal outcomes & cost savings of drug and alcohol treatment in the State of Oregon*. Salem, OR: Office of Alcohol and Drug Abuse Programs, Oregon Department of Human Resources and Governor's Council on Alcohol and Drug Abuse Programs.

Gerstein, D. R., Johnson, R. A., Harwood, H., Fountain, D., Suter, N., & Malloy, K. (1994). *Evaluating recovery services: The California drug and alcohol treatment assessment*. Sacramento, CA: California Department of Alcohol and Drug Programs.

Langenbucher, J. W., McCrady, B. S., Brick, J., & Esterly, R. (1994). *Socioeconomic evaluations of addictions treatment*. Piscataway, NJ: Center on Alcohol Studies, Rutgers University.

Leshner, A. (1994). A comprehensive strategy for improving drug abuse treatment. *Journal of Substance Abuse Treatment, 11* (6), 483-486.

Magura, S., Laudet, A. I., Kange, S. Y., & Whitney, S. (1998). *Effectiveness of comprehensive services for crack-dependent mothers with newborns and young children*. New York: National Development and Research Institutes, Inc.

McLellan, A., Metzger, D. A., Alterman, A. I., Woody, G. E., Durell, J., & O'Brien, C. P. (1995). *Is addiction treatment "worth it"? Public health expectations, policy-based comparisons*. Philadelphia, PA: The Penn-VA Center for Studies on Addiction and the Treatment Research Institute.

Mee-Lee, D. (1995). Matching in addictions treatment: How do we get there from here? In N.S. Miller (Ed.). *Treatment of the addictions: Applications of outcomes research for clinical management* (pp. 113-127). New York: The Haworth Press.

Morgan, T. J. (1996). Behavioral treatment techniques for psychoactive substance use disorders. In F. Rogters, D. W. Keller, & J. Morgenstern (Eds.), *Treating substance abuse: Theory and technique* (pp. 202-240). New York: The Guilford Press.

Meuller, M. D., & Wyman, J. R. (1997). Study sheds new light on the state of drug abuse treatment nationwide. *NIDA Notes.* 12(5): 1, 4-8.

National Association for Children of Alcoholics. (1997). *Core competencies for involvement of health care providers in the care of children and adolescents in families affected by substance abuse.* New York: Author.

Prochaska, J. O., & DiClemente, C. C. (1985). Toward a comprehensive model of change. In W. R. Miller & N. Health (Eds.), *Treating addictive behaviors: Processes of change.* New York: Plenum Press.

Richardson, B., & Weinstein, N. (1997). *Support groups that work.* New York: Children of Alcoholics Foundation.

Substance Abuse and Mental Health Services Administration [SAMHSA], Center for Substance Abuse Treatment. (1997). *National treatment improvement evaluation study summary.* Rockville, MD: U.S. Department of Health and Human Services, Center for Substance Abuse Treatment. Details of the study can be downloaded from the CSAT website at http://www.health.org/nties97.

Vega, P. (1998). Disease management: Moving from fledgling concept to revolution in behavioral health care. *Behavioral Disease Management Report.* Providence, RI: Manisses Publications.

U.S. Department of Health and Human Services [DHHS], Public Health Services, Substance Abuse and Mental Health Services Administration. (1995). *Effectiveness of substance abuse treatment.* DHHS Publication No (SMA) 95-3067: 37-44. Washington, DC: U.S. Department of Health and Human Services.

Young, N. K., & Gardner, S. L. (1997). *Implementing welfare reform.* Washington, DC: Drug Strategies and Irvine, CA: Children and Family Futures.

Waltman, D. (1995). Key ingredients to effective addictions treatment. *Journal of Substance Abuse Treatment*, 12(6), 429-439.

5

Assessment:
Bridging Child Welfare and AOD Services

Throughout this guidebook, as we have examined the experience gained by the model projects (especially Sacramento's AODTI), we have stressed the importance of improved methods of assessing child safety and AOD treatment needs. This chapter discusses assessment and its importance to the process of developing closer links in responding to AOD-CWS problems.

Child welfare service professionals face many difficult challenges in carrying out their responsibilities. Each day they make critical decisions in assessing the safety of children who are at risk of maltreatment and in determining when children must be placed in out-of-home care to ensure their safety. A further function of CWS is to identify short- and long-term services that are needed to enhance the well-being of children and families. To help guide such important and difficult decisions, child welfare agencies have developed various screening and risk assessment practices and procedures. Indeed, in a recent series of meetings between child welfare agency professionals and AOD treatment administrators in California, assessment was the area of daily practice that received the greatest attention [Gardner & Young 1997].

The words "risk assessment" and "assessment" are used in ways that are sometimes confusing. CWS agencies conduct risk assessment, but many are also involved in broader assessments of family strengths, concerns, and needs of children and families that go beyond the immediate risks to a child.* Risk assessment generally refers to near-term threats to a child, while the broader conception of family assessment refers to the more comprehensive, long-term needs.

---

* An excellent new source that clarifies these distinctions in more detail, as well as addressing the issues in this section of our paper in considerable depth, is a new CWLA publication, *Ours to Keep*. Day, P., Robison, S. & Sheikh, L. (1998).

Discussion has intensified about how to strengthen risk assessment strategies, but many policymakers and service personnel still lack adequate understanding of the risk to a child resulting from a parent's substance use. In practice, most CWS administrators view substance abuse as simply one more component of risk and do not devote specific attention or resources to understanding its threat to children in proportion to the incidence of AOD problems in their caseloads or its co-occurrence with family violence, mental illness, and employment problems.

Risk assessment protocols need to better integrate and link the best practices of child welfare services with those of AOD treatment agencies. Blending risk assessment in the child protective services system with the screening and assessment of AOD problems is an essential step to help ensure the well-being of children and families for two key reasons:

- *Risk assessment is the core of daily practice in both the child welfare and AOD systems.* It is the process by which critical judgments related to child safety and the need for and progress in AOD treatment services are made.

- *Family assessment serves as a primary leverage point for helping strengthen families who enter the child welfare system.* The process presents workers with some of their most important choices in determining the approach they will take with their clients.

The Basic Premises

Two premises inform this section, which should be made explicit:

- Assessing AOD problems is integral to the process of assessing risk to children and family functioning. It should not be seen as an optional add-on—it is part of the core of the basic process of assessing risk, as fundamental as the question of whether the family has been reported in prior incidents or looking for signs of physical abuse on the children.

- Within the child welfare system, it is possible and necessary to assess the level of AOD problems in enough depth to make a "good handoff"—to refer a client with a much better chance of getting treatment resources, because the referral comes with enough information about the CWS client to know what kind of services they need from the AOD system. Both AOD and CWS systems would view this as a major change, and not all agencies will agree with this premise.

The Problem

It is important to be clear about the shortcomings of the current screening and assessment process in CPS as it addresses AOD issues. There are three separable issues:

- *Screening for AOD problems is cursory and not standardized.* It usually involves a single question that the worker answers using subjective factors and her intuition. But without AOD training, a worker may find it hard to be objective in the case and to be able to interpret the subtle signs of AOD problems. When an attempt is made to use objective criteria, what is often used instead of a more thorough screening is the simple marker of a urine toxicological screen, which has many limitations, including the lack of any indication of severity of the AOD problem, since it only indicates recent use of some substances that can be reliably detected. More detailed screening is essential; not seeing drug paraphernalia, for example, is not an indication that there are no pervasive alcohol problems in the family.

- *Without standardized information in the file that includes reports on screening for AOD use, abuse, and dependence, it becomes impossible to weigh the importance of AOD factors for a single case or across thousands of cases in a*

regression analysis designed to revise risk assessment tools.
Testing the models of risk, as has been proposed by several CWS agencies, leaves out the measures of one of the
conditions that affects risk, which is AOD problems. The
computer adage GIGO comes to mind: "garbage in, garbage out"— meaning that if it isn't entered into the file in
the first place, finding a correlation between AOD abuse
and risks to children is clearly impossible.

Here is where an important caveat is needed: As much as
we believe that AOD screening and assessment should be
expanded in the CPS process, we should not advocate for
that expansion with a guarantee that it will lead directly
to foolproof detection of dangerous abuse and neglect. We
simply do not know enough yet about the connection between these obviously related factors to make that prom-
ise, in part because the issue has not been seen important
enough for useful data to be collected over time. This is
similar to the issues raised in the last section about the
credibility of treatment itself—if we overstate the impact
with excessive claims for effectiveness that cannot be supported, we will lose credibility.

- *When AOD abuse is detected, the typical referral to AOD
  treatment is not based on an assessment of the severity of
  the problem or the level of treatment needed to respond to
  the problem.* The typical referral, as discussed in Chapter
  1, is a set of phone numbers of treatment centers or a call
  to the AOD agency to which a CPS client is referred without any detail as to the nature of the problem or the recommended level of treatment. Making an assessment of
  the AOD problem is not seen as a part of the basic CWS
  mission—it is the responsibility of the AOD agency and
  so a phone number of the local treatment agency is seen as
  enough to get the case over into that system. This often

"You're Making Lousy Referrals"

In one community where CWS and AOD staff have been making a genuine, good faith effort to work together more effectively, the dialogue in the early stages of their discussions became fairly heated, with AOD workers saying to their CWS counterparts "You're making lousy referrals, sending us people who don't want treatment at all, with no information for us about their problems, and then expecting us to do something with them."

---

results in a backlog on the AOD side and a failure of the CWS client to negotiate the gap between the two systems.

Once referral is made from CWS to AOD agency, the "layering" of assessment takes place, in which CPS assessment is followed by AOD assessment in a totally separate process. This can frustrate the client and the frontline worker, as repetitious questions are asked and answered. (In following the recommendations of this report and others with regard to family violence and mental health, the layering problem can become even more severe, with each of these agencies requiring its own, completely separate process on top of all the other ones.)

Responses to the Problem

- Screening for AOD problems should be a standard element of every CPS risk assessment and, of equal importance, should go beyond the single-question approach to include at least (1) a CAGE-type brief screening (described below) for the presence of AOD problems, and (2) a differentiation between use, abuse, and dependence, as a SASSI-type diagnostic tool can do. Some agencies would add the key markers that in their local experience strongly correlate with risk, such as stimulant use and heavy alcohol use associated with a history of violence.

- Following this level of screening, if positive for AOD problems, the CWS worker should use the family assessment to determine how AOD factors are affecting the needs of the family across all the domains in which AOD factors may be at work, including health, employment history, legal problems, parenting styles, etc. Knowing that a parent is chemically dependent should lead to the obvious question of how that affects the areas of life in that family—how severe are those problems and what kind of services are needed to address those problems?

If the head of the household has been unemployed for a lengthy period, taking AOD issues seriously would obviously lead to asking whether AOD use contributes to the job history. Yet many family assessment tools would merely record the fact of the job history and not seek to link it to the AOD problems, if any. In effect, what is needed is a kind of engagement of the client around AOD issues that raises—perhaps for the first time for some clients—the connections between AOD abuse and life events. The consequences of AOD abuse in the client's life may become clearer, and the basis for treatment may become more powerful as well. This can be seen as motivational interviewing connected with AOD assessment, as discussed in Chapter 2.

With this information, a CWS worker can negotiate the AOD system, knowing what kind of relapse history, needs for program, structure needs, or time limits in TANF are affecting this client. The worker is then armed with the information she needs on how to negotiate the AOD system on behalf of her client. The AOD system should then collect information on baselines for treatment planning that is linked with the family plan in the CWS system, relying on information from CWS on the severity of the problem and the full range of biopsychosocial issues.

If the entire AOD assessment happens over in the AOD system, as proposed by some CWS agencies, the disconnect from CWS may make it far more difficult to ensure that the full needs of the family can be met, since the AOD system will not weigh those needs as heavily as the CWS system might. Integrating AOD-related assessment with existing CWS screening and assessments ensures that parents' first point of contact is with a CWS worker who is able to make an informed and in-depth judgment about clients' AOD problems, which leads in turn to much greater likelihood that those needs can be met in the AOD system, based on a better "handoff" from CWS to AOD.

The Changing Nature of Assessment

Initially, child protective service agencies investigated reports of child maltreatment with the primary intent of *substantiating* whether a specific incident of abuse occurred. Increasingly, states are trying to shift their philosophical focus from one of "investigations and policing" to assessing family needs and providing appropriate services [DePanfilis & Scannapieco 1994]. Child welfare agencies are seeking to establish a different kind of relationship with the families they see—one that is collaborative and supportive, based on the family strengths, rather than contentious and punitive, focused only on the family's deficits.

Both CWS and AOD agencies have begun to refine their screening and assessment processes to differentiate between functions within the systems. Child welfare agencies are looking at assessment in a broader framework that ties assessment practices to effective case planning and management of agency resources. Iowa's legislation, for example, states that while the primary purpose of an assessment is protection of the child's safety, the secondary purpose is "to engage the child's family in services to enhance family strengths and address needs" [Christian 1997].

In the AOD field, screening and assessment are also increasingly being viewed as distinct functions. Screening determines whether a client has an AOD-related problem and assessment determines which aspects of the client's life are affected by AOD use, abuse, or dependence. These areas of life functioning generally include patterns of alcohol use, characteristics of other drug use, physical problems, social relationships, family problems, legal problems and criminal behavior, psychological problems, environmental conditions including housing and community safety, and employment or economic support problems. The more physical, psychological, and social problems a person experiences, the more intensive and structured their early recovery experiences need to be, as described above in discussing treatment.

CWS and AOD Assessment Processes and Tools

Both the CWS and AOD assessment and screening processes are complex, with varying definitions and different tools used for different purposes. Similarities across the two systems do exist, however, as shown in Table 11, with three discrete phases of the larger screening and assessment process.

CWS Risk Assessment Methods

Within the variety of risk assessment protocols is a wide range of assessment instruments. Some assess the immediate safety of the child, others help predict future maltreatment, and still others are designed to inform decisions about out-of-home care and family preservation. Models used by Illinois, California, Florida, Michigan, Missouri, New York, Texas, Washington, and Wisconsin are commonly cited in the risk assessment literature, as well as tools that address broader issues of family functioning and child well-being, such as the Child Well-Being Scales, Family Risk Scales, Family Assessment Form, Children at Risk Field, and Child Abuse Potential Inventory.

AOD Assessment Methods

Similar to the CWS system, AOD agencies use a number of different assessment methods and tools to screen and assess for AOD-related problems among juveniles, adults in the criminal justice system, hospitalized trauma patients, and others. The two *screening* tools referred to in this chapter are the CAGE questionnaire (described in Table 12 on page 126) and the Substance Abuse Subtle Screening Inventory (SASSI). Frequently used assessment tools include the Addiction Severity Index (ASI), the American Society of Addiction Medicine (ASAM) Patient Placement Criteria, and the Individual Assessment Profile (IAP).

Extensive research has been conducted on screening and assessment instruments used in the AOD field, but no tools exist that were designed specifically for rating the risk of child abuse or neglect in terms of parental substance abuse. Most existing instruments there-

Table 11. The Phases of the Screening and Assessment Process

Child Welfare System	AOD Treatment System
• *Safety Assessment*—to determine the degree of *immediate* danger of maltreatment to the child	• *Safety Screening*—to identify if there is an AOD problem and whether an individual requires immediate attention
• *Risk Assessment*—to assess the likelihood that child is at risk of near-term abuse and/or neglect and the appropriate CWS programmatic response	• *Patient Treatment Placement*—to determine level of client functioning for the appropriate level of intensity and structure that is needed by the individual
• *Psychosocial Assessment/Family Functioning Assessment*—to evaluate the *long-term* risks to the child and develop and implement appropriate interventions and case plans for the family based on their strengths and needs	• *Psychosocial Needs Assessment*—to determine how AOD affects areas of life functioning and to develop case plans for specialized care and appropriate interventions

fore have limited use for families in the child welfare system [Olsen et al. 1996]. In both CWS and AOD fields, each state (or in some states, each county or provider) determines in its own unique way whether or not to adopt a particular protocol [Kern & Sheets 1996].

In fact, a recent survey of state public child welfare agencies by the Child Welfare League of America (CWLA) found that no more than 6% of the responding agencies use a standardized test such as the SASSI or Drug Use Screening Inventory (DUSI) to screen for alcohol and other drug use. Close to one-third (32%) said they use some "other" kind of tool when screening for AOD, and 11% reported that they used locally developed instruments [CWLA 1997].

One encouraging example of an instrument that assesses child abuse/neglect risk in AOD-abusing families was developed in Rhode Island. The Risk Inventory for Substance Abuse-Affected Families [Children's Friend & Service 1994] was developed by the staff of Project Connect, a home-based program serving families with substance abuse problems. The Inventory consists of eight scales, each of which is anchored by either four or five descriptive statements that define corresponding levels of risk. Workers complete the inventory after conducting an initial assessment of the family and collecting all relevant data needed for case planning. Five of the eight scales focus directly on substance abuse issues and are presented below; three assess how a parent's self-efficacy, self-care, and quality of neighborhood may also affect the level of risk to the child:

- *Parent's commitment to recovery.* This scale assesses parents' stages of recovery, their willingness to change behavior, and their desire to live a life free from alcohol and other drugs.

- *Patterns of substance use.* This scale assesses the parent's patterns of alcohol and other drug use ranging from active use without regard to consequences to significant periods of abstinence.

- *Effect of substance use on child caring.* This scale assesses a parent's ability to care for his/her children and meet the child's emotional and physical needs.

- *Effect of substance use on lifestyle.* This scale assesses a parent's ability to carry out his/her everyday responsibilities and any consequences that may have for the family.

- *Support for recovery:* assesses parent's social network and how that network may support or interfere with recovery.

Challenges to Implementing a Linked CWS-AOD Assessment Strategy

Despite recent progress, successfully implementing risk assessment models has proven difficult [Kern & Sheets 1996]. Listed below are some of the key challenges to incorporating AOD elements in risk assessment models:

- *Difficulty in operationalizing risk to children.* No standard or accepted indicator determines how or when parents' use of alcohol or other drugs becomes an increased risk factor to children [Day et al. 1998]. Our review of many risk assessment protocols found that there is no universal approach to ranking the risk that parental AOD abuse poses to children. In interpreting risk along the AOD continuum of use, abuse, and dependence, signs such as positive toxicology screens, birth of an AOD-exposed infant, or a prior child maltreatment incident involving use of alcohol or other drugs are at times difficult to interpret in relationship to child risk. Other AOD signs tend to be imprecise—examples of vague terms that need to be more clearly defined are "periodically" incapable of caring for the child (how often?); "reduced" ability to parent (to what extent?); or "discernible effect" on user or family (what kind of effect?).

- *Concerns about excessive caseloads.* Many child welfare practitioners and administrators have expressed concern that improved assessments will lead to an increased demand for AOD services that simply do not exist now and will not be funded. As a member of a multicounty group of AOD and CWS officials put it: "'Don't ask, don't tell' is a policy that protects the system from collapse."

- *Competency and training of staff.* Child welfare practitioners are typically ill-prepared to identify and respond to families where substance abuse is the predominant problem. Without skills in interviewing, assessment, decision making, time management, and other important competency areas related to AOD-using clients, even the best systems will not be effective [Depanfilis 1996].

- *Values and attitudes.* The best risk assessment system is not a good system unless workers will use it; attitudes about the importance of risk assessment within the child welfare system vary widely from site to site. Some states, for example, assign their best staff to the assessment process on the grounds that the screening decision is one of the most important that CWS will make, while others regard screening as a clerical function [Rosenkrantz & Waldfogel 1996]. Previous studies have documented that child welfare workers may discount the utility of risk assessment systems, refuse to use them, or complete the paperwork *after* making case decisions [Johnson 1996]. Nor is there a solid consensus on the need to step up efforts to screen for AOD problems in the risk assessment process. Some officials view AOD issues as simply one of several conditions that need to be assessed, while others worry that policymakers may adopt an extreme stance that declares that AOD abuse by parents always equates to child abuse, when in fact some individuals use alcohol and other drugs without putting their children at demonstrable significant risk of abuse or neglect [Young & Gardner 1997].

Though risk assessment can result in a meaningful snapshot that describes a family's situation and needs, it is rare that risk assessment findings form the basis for shared decision making across agency boundaries or promote increased collaboration on cases [Schene 1996]. Instead, what we find is that each agency involved with a family demands its own separate assessment by its own workers.

Unless AOD assessments are integrated with CWS assessments, multiple layers of assessments will be created for a myriad of issues each treated separately and assessed categorically. The result is an overburdened CWS system that addresses clients' needs in a fragmented rather than coherent manner. With the vast majority of CWS cases affected by AOD, there needs to be an understanding that risk assessment can and should include an AOD treatment needs assessment. This understanding requires a fundamental shift in prevailing CWS approaches, which currently work to screen out AOD problems, rather than acknowledging them and directly addressing them.

This shift would demand that risk assessment lead to early, accurate, and informed decisions regarding what kind of AOD services would be most appropriate and effective for the *whole* family [Young & Gardner 1997]. A prime opportunity exists to join together with other agencies and other disciplines serving children and families to develop risk assessment models that are more powerful and address the wide range of needs of families and children in the child welfare system [Kern & Sheets 1996].

The assessment process must go the extra step to actually connect clients to treatment programs, rather than simply "refer out" with a phone number of the nearest treatment agency. As one CWS official put it: "We need to cross the border between assessments and treatment. We act at times as if we do the SASSI and then we have solved the AOD issues" [Young & Gardner 1997]. Stronger ties through the assessment process between the CWS and AOD systems will help ensure that treatment is more likely to be available on demand to parents with the motivation and support to succeed in treatment. Better linkages between CWS and AOD agencies will enable clearer targeting of CWS clients for treatment and monitoring progress of parents, and help in making critical decisions about child safety.

What this kind of assessment would mean is a major shift from the concern of CWS assessment with *immediate risk to the safety of the child* to a wider concern for the *overall risk to the child's well-being*. As Jacquelyn McCroskey and others have pointed out, this is—or should be—the essential difference between CPS and CWS: a deeper concern for family functioning that goes beyond immediate risk to the larger issue of how AOD problems affect the entire family. Without this wider concern, the immediate risk perspective will lead to CPS caring only about the most extreme cases of AOD abuse, rather than the more profound issues of how AOD abuse, family violence, mental health, and family income support are all affecting children and family functioning [McCroskey 1998].

Leverage Points That Promote Connection

To link CWS and AOD assessment practices requires a deeper understanding of the decision points at each of the three phases for both systems. This will help inform which elements of AOD screening need to be incorporated at any given point in the larger assessment process. Though assessment by itself will not integrate the two systems, there are several important starting points where the two systems can intersect in serving clients that need both sets of services.

Screen all families for AOD problems. Within CWS, there needs to be an explicit assumption that AOD abuse and dependence pose a risk to children's safety and therefore should become a formal, deliberate, and expanded part of the CWS screening and assessment process. Some experts have even suggested the need for mandatory substance abuse screening in all cases of serious child abuse and neglect [Murphy 1991].

Strengthen workers' capacity with more appropriate assessment tools. Workers describe families so devastated by drugs that "risk" is constant and impossible to assess [CWLA 1991]. This task becomes even more difficult given the shortcomings of traditional CWS assessment tools. Furthermore, the more subtle indicators of AOD problems (such as health problems or impaired social functioning associated with dependence) are "clues easily overlooked when relying on a general risk assessment instrument" [Dore et al. 1995].

Assess for family strengths as well as problems. As CWS agencies step up their efforts to screen for AOD problems, they must remember to explore AOD in a broader context of family functioning. In particular, child welfare workers need to become more knowledgeable and balanced in assessing AOD abuse and its relationship to other issues and strengths in the family [Cole et al. 1996]. Cole and her colleagues caution: "The most damaging consequence of a preoccupation with the pathology of substance abuse is that family strengths are rarely identified or given the weight they deserve" [1996].

Broaden the lens through which AOD problems are viewed. The child protection system needs to broaden its focus on AOD issues in at least three fundamental ways.

- More attention must be focused on the significance of alcohol abuse—not just illicit drug use—and its effects on children. In addition, given the increasing body of evidence on the prenatal impact of nicotine, both of these legal drugs should be addressed in greater depth.

• More emphasis must be placed on children affected by parental AOD abuse *after* birth. The attention given to services and supports for prenatally exposed infants is well justified, but many of the children environmentally exposed to AOD may be at higher risk for more severe consequences.

• The CWS system needs to accept more responsibility for the families who clearly have AOD problems but are screened out because they do not warrant formal investigations, or the investigation has been unable to substantiate the allegation. Without proper intervention, these families are likely to return as "high-risk" cases. This is an appropriate role for the community partnership models described in Chapter 2.

So the task is as clear as it is difficult: combining risk assessment in the CWS system with screening and assessment of AOD problems and combining assessment of an individual's AOD-related problems with measures of family functioning and risk to the children. In the CWS system, the threshold issue is whether to add an explicit assumption that AOD abuse and dependence always poses a risk to the child and therefore should become a formal, deliberate, and expanded part of the screening and assessment process in child protective services. If so, should levels of risk to the child be differentiated in terms of specific drugs, frequency of use, changes in behavior in association with use, or AOD use in conjunction with other high-risk situations (e.g., an unrelated male in a caretaker role who has a history of AOD problems or of violence)? We propose that the functions within CWS can be viewed in terms of their current assessment protocols and that specific AOD-related content must be added to these existing assessment processes. These are summarized in Table 12.

Table 12. Assessment Processes with AOD Considerations

CWS Phase	CWS Function	CWS Methods	Suggested AOD Content
Initial response to allegation of abuse or neglect	Investigate allegation of abuse or neglect	Risk assessment protocols measures such factors as the following: • Child (e.g., vulnerability, behavior) • Child abuse/neglect incident • Parent characteristics (e.g., parenting skills, mental health, history of abuse) • Parent-child interaction (e.g., attitude toward and expectations for child) • Family and social relationships (e.g., family violence, family stressors, crises) • Living environment (e.g., financial security, housing status) • Motivation to change behavior (e.g., willingness to cooperate with agencies) • General demographic factors	Simple screening questions, such as a modified CAGE: • Have you ever felt you should CUT DOWN on your drinking or drug abuse? • Have people ANNOYED you by criticizing or complaining about your drinking or drug use? • Have you ever felt bad or GUILTY about your drinking or drug use? • Have you ever had a drink or drug in the morning (EYE OPENER) to steady your nerves or to get rid of a hangover? • Do you use any drugs other than those prescribed by a physician? • Has a physician ever told you to cut down or quit the use of alcohol or drugs? • Has your drinking/drug use caused family, job, or legal problems? • When drinking/using drug, have you had a memory loss (blackout)? ✓ Two or more affirmative responses indicate with high likelihood that the person is a problem drinker and/or a drug abuser and requires further assessment.
	Determine risk to the child(ren)	Further analysis of risk assessment protocols and interviews with key informants.	Information on the type and frequency of substance abuse: • Is there use of stimulants (e.g., cocaine, crack, methamphetamine)? • Is the use of heavy alcohol accompanied by a history of violence? ✓ If yes, there is potential for higher risk to the child.

CWS Phase	CWS Function	CWS Methods	Suggested AOD Content
Triage and CWS program placement based on risk to the child	Determine if there is legal basis for petition and appropriate placement	Preparation of court report through review of CWS history, risk assessment, interview statement of child, parents, relatives, law enforcement, etc.	Discriminate between substance use, abuse, or dependence: • Diagnostic tools, such as the Substance Abuse Subtle Screening Inventory. • DSM-IV diagnostic criteria ✓ If substance abuse present, case requires further AOD-specific services and information should be evaluated in the CWS program placement decision.
Case planning and management	Create a service plan, provide referrals/service linkages Monitor progress Reassess and document progress Make decisions regarding case disposition	Assessment of such psychosocial and family functioning factors as the following: • Physical environment (e.g., housing) • Social environment (e.g., family support systems) • Financial environment • Caregivers' history • Personal characteristics • Child-rearing skills • Child(ren)'s developmental status • Child(ren)'s behavior • Interpersonal interactions among adults • Interpersonal interactions among adults and child(ren)	Determine appropriate AOD treatment services and areas of life functioning affected by AOD use (domains of the ASI): • Medical problems • Legal problems • Social problems • Family problems • Psychological problems • Employment/education problems • Treatment acceptance/resistance ✓ Use information on levels of functioning to make appropriate AOD treatment decisions regarding level of structure or intensity of services required and areas of life functioning requiring specific interventions in the treatment plan.

Guiding Principles for Effective Assessment

Clearly, improved risk assessment methods are needed to help child welfare workers make efficient and accurate decisions concerning AOD-involved families. Our experiences in cities across the country, together with a review of the relevant literature, point to a set of guiding principles for child welfare agencies as they seek to develop a blended CWS-AOD assessment strategy that includes risk assessment, but goes beyond it to a wider review of the family's overall capacity to deal with substance abuse and other problems.

Guiding Principles for Developing an Integrated
CWS-AOD Assessment Approach

- Address both the problem of AOD use and child maltreatment.

- Assess the interaction between AOD use, abuse, or dependence, and child maltreatment, and what it means for risk to the child.

- Establish standards for intervention that relate explicitly to assessment(s), including appropriate level of AOD intervention(s).

- Include assessment of strengths inherent in the family, which leads to an appropriate service/treatment plan for the family as a whole.

- Conduct assessments in the broader context of overall family functioning and behavior (e.g., use and availability of support systems and community resources, desire and capacity to parent, child's attachment to the family, child's special medical/developmental needs) [Tracy & Farkas 1994].

- Develop assessment protocols that are sensitive to cultural, ethnic-, and gender-related concerns.

- View any assessment instrument as a tool to enhance—not substitute for—professional clinical judgment.

- Consider family violence, mental health, and job readiness assessments as part of related systems that affect CWS-AOD outcomes

- Link assessments to workload and budgeting—supervisors, managers, policymakers, budget analysts, and others should use assessment information about the levels of clients' needs to help manage agency resources and net increases in paperwork should be avoided.

References

Child Welfare League of America. (1997). *Alcohol and other drug survey of state child welfare agencies.* Washington, DC: Author.

Children's Friend and Service. (1994). *Risk inventory for substance abuse-affected families.* Providence, RI: Author.

Christian, S. (1997). *New directions for child protective services: Supporting children, families, and communities through legislative reform.* Denver, CO: National Conference on State Legislatures.

Cole, E., Barth, R., Crocker, A., & Moss, K. (1996). *Policy and practice challenges in serving infants and young children whose parents abuse drugs and alcohol.* Boston, MA: Family Builders Network.

Day, P., Robison, S., & Sheikh. L. (1998). *Ours to keep: Building a community risk assessment strategy for child protection.* Washington, DC: CWLA Press.

DePanfilis, D. (1996). Implementing child mistreatment risk assessment systems: Lessons from theory. *Administration in Social Work, 20*(2), 41-59.

DePanfilis, D., & Scannapieco, M. (1994). Assessing the safety of children at risk of maltreatment: Decision-making models. *Child Welfare*, 73 (3), 229-245.

Dore, M. M., Doris, J., & Wright, P. (1995). Identifying substance abuse in maltreating families: A child welfare challenge. *Child Abuse and Neglect*, 19(5), 531-543.

Gardner, S., & Young, N. (1997). *Bridge building: An action plan for state and county efforts to strengthen links between child welfare services and services for alcohol and other drug problems.* Irvine, CA: Children and Family Futures.

Johnson, W. (1996). Risk assessment research: Progress and future directions. *Protecting Children*, 12(2), 14-19.

Kern, H., & Sheets, D. (1996). Our knowledge is imperfect, but we're working on it and we're learning: A state perspective on risk assessment—past, present, and future. *Protecting Children*, 12(2), 20-23.

McCroskey, J. (March 1998). Personal communication.

Murphy, J. M., Jellinek, M., Quinn, D., Smith, G., Poitrast, F., & Goshko, M. (1991). Substance abuse and serious maltreatment: Prevalence, risk and outcome in a court sample. *Child Abuse and Neglect*, 15, 197-211.

Olsen, L., Allen, D., & Azzi-Lessing, L. (1996). Assessing risk in families affected by substance abuse. *Child Abuse and Neglect*, 20(9), 833-842.

Rosenkrantz, S., & Waldfogel, J. (1996). *Reporting, screening and investigation of child maltreatment: Entry into the child protective services system.* Cambridge, MA: Malcolm Weiner Center for Social Policy and Program in Criminal Justice Policy and Management, John F. Kennedy School of Government, Harvard University.

Schene, P. (1996). The risk assessment roundtables: A ten-year perspective. *Protecting Children*, 12(2), 4-8.

Tracy, E., & Farkas, K. (1994). Preparing practitioners for child welfare practice with substance- abusing families. *Child Welfare*, 73(1), 57-68.

6

Beyond the Boundaries of Child Welfare:
Connecting with Welfare, Juvenile Justice, Family Violence, and Mental Health Systems

As noted in the Introduction, several service systems outside the parameters of child welfare affect and are affected by AOD problems among children and families. Agencies in the domains of welfare reform, juvenile justice, family violence, and mental health are, at various stages, participants in the identification, assessment, and prevention/treatment of problems among children and families affected by substance abuse. CWS practitioners have also emphasized the importance of school systems, primary health agencies, law enforcement, and housing agencies in meeting the needs of CWS families with AOD problems. Child welfare officials must acknowledge that these other systems are essential players in addressing AOD problems faced by children and families. This section describes the existing overlap of cases among these systems, highlighting the interrelated nature of these problems and their solutions, which often require services from systems other than AOD and child welfare.

The Link to TANF

The overlap of AOD problems with welfare caseloads underscores the importance of addressing poverty as well as the other underlying factors in child welfare caseloads [Young & Gardner 1997]. A recent work that has masterfully woven together the three policy arenas of human services reform, community organizing, and community economic development is *Building Community*, by Bruner and Parachini [1997]. Many practitioners would add a greater emphasis upon community or neighborhood development to efforts to build community partnerships for child welfare services, following the conclusions of a massive study of community prevention programs commissioned by the Office of Justice programs in the U.S. Department of Justice:

> ...community prevention programs address none of [the] causes of community composition and structure, which in turn influence community culture and the availability of criminogenic substances like guns and drugs [Sherman et al. 1997].

Predictions in some states that welfare cuts will affect CWS caseloads have led to efforts to look more closely at the effects of the 1996 welfare reform legislation on children. A series of federally and foundation-funded efforts based in a select group of states are monitoring the impact of welfare changes on the children of TANF recipients, including assessments of child welfare impact [Christian 1997]. With the recently announced decline of welfare caseloads to below the level of 10,000,000 for the first time since 1970, information on the effects of these reductions on CWS caseloads becomes critical, especially those for child neglect. Judith Gueron of the Manpower Demonstration Research Corporation, which is conducting studies in Minnesota and Florida, stated in January 1998 that "about half of the people leaving welfare are employed, and half are not" [Pear 1998]. The second group is the portion in which monitoring child neglect would seem critically important, since neglect is already making up a majority of CPS cases in most states.

A possible problem arises from the traditional separation between income support and child welfare programs. Though often placed within the same agency, the two systems have tended to seek different goals: the welfare system seeks the removal of parents from welfare and the child welfare system focuses upon children who may be endangered. With different eligibility rules, and now with different ideas of entitlement and time limits, the two systems will only work together effectively if these barriers can be overcome in family-centered approaches that take a wider view of clients' needs and strengths.

As noted in our earlier work on TANF, it appears likely that as caseloads decline in number, clients with more severe barriers to employment will be encountered more frequently, requiring a wider array of assessment and support services.

The Juvenile Justice Connection

The problems of substance-abusing parents of children are not confined to the domains of child welfare and welfare systems for some families—they extend further to impact the juvenile justice system. As CWLA notes: "The courts, like the child welfare system, are in crisis—overwhelmed by ... increasing numbers of cases involving alcohol and other drug abuse" [CWLA 1992: p. 97]. Yet, there exists a major disconnect between the child welfare and juvenile justice systems.

Recognizing the need for stronger linkages, participants at a recent Office of Juvenile Justice and Delinquency Prevention (OJJDP) conference concluded that "one large system" was needed to meet these families' complex needs. The conference summary captures the essence of the problem:

> Because abuse and dependency have root causes in dysfunctional families and unfavorable environments, and because being abused engenders the mental and emotional turmoil likely to lead to delinquency, child welfare and juvenile justice professionals end up working with many of the same kids [OJJDP 1997].

Why the Juvenile Justice Connection Is Critical

Research on the relationship between childhood maltreatment and subsequent adolescent problem behaviors provides clear evidence of the need for child welfare services and juvenile justice to work in tandem. Findings from the Rochester Youth Development Study, for instance, indicated that children who were abused or neglected were significantly more likely to engage in serious and violent delinquency. Forty-five percent of maltreated youth, compared to less than one-third (32%) of nonmaltreated youth, had official records of delinquency. Maltreated children were also at increased risk of other interrelated problems in adolescence including drug use, poor academic performance, teen pregnancy, and emotional and mental health disorders [Kelley et al. 1997].

In 1997, Sacramento County planned the Community Intervention Project to link juvenile justice and child welfare service agencies. Sacramento implemented this effort in response to research conducted by CWLA that found the following:

- Approximately 2% of the 75,000 children age 9 to 12 in Sacramento County were known to the child welfare system,

- More than one-half of those children (56%) were arrested for juvenile offenses, and

- These youth were far more likely to continue committing serious offenses, based on the early age of their first involvement with the juvenile justice system [Morgan & Gutterman 1995].

The Sacramento initiative targets these high-risk youth and their families in an intensive effort to prevent their continued involvement with the justice system.

Early intervention with these preadolescents has become a clear priority for some innovative juvenile justice agencies. Yet as these children grow older, they obviously begin to be perceived, within their own community and the larger society as well, as more dangerous than endangered. As the OJJDP study on childhood maltreatment noted:

> When a child victim becomes a juvenile offender, legitimate concerns about protecting public safety and holding youth accountable for their behavior can overshadow issues of continued trauma from childhood maltreatment ... Punitive responses ... may exacerbate previous emotional and developmental problems resulting from maltreatment [Kelley et al. 1997].

The response of the juvenile justice system to the needs of these children has been mixed, like that of other systems for which AOD issues have been treated as a side current to the mainstream of services. Exemplary practice is visible in a few agencies and general disregard for the problems of AOD abuse in many others. As stated in a recent CSAT report on AOD treatment for adolescents diverted from the juvenile justice system:

> Although juvenile courts historically have functioned within a network of community social service and treatment agencies, these networks' responsiveness to AOD-abusing youth has at best inconsistently met the needs of courts, youth, and families. Many AOD abuse treatment programs were developed to serve only those adolescents and families who seek help [McPhail & West 1995].

This report goes on to recommend a strategy for diverting appropriate youth from the juvenile justice system to AOD treatment agencies, capitalizing on three opportunities:

- The access of the juvenile justice system to AOD intervention and treatment when needed;

- The capacity of the AOD treatment agencies to use the authority of the court to encourage compliance; and

- The capacity of multiple agencies working together to provide a continuum of services to specific youths, including AOD treatment, physical health, mental health, and other social services, based on the youth's individual, multiple needs for treatment and other services.

The guidelines for these diversion programs emphasize the nature of AOD abuse as a family disease and thus require family involvement whenever possible. Conventional definitions of family may not apply in all youths' situations and at times a supportive adult, who may or may not be a birth parent, may be a critical factor. These guidelines also stress that adolescent clients may require different treatment services from those of adult AOD abusers, including specialized education, pre-employment training, leisure activities, and mentoring.

Finally, we cannot lose sight of the older youth who are, in effect, "graduates" of the child welfare system. In some cases these youth, who were often abused or neglected as younger children, have become involved in dysfunctional and criminal behavior as users, distributors, and sellers of drugs, and thus represent disruptive forces within their own families. These youth are far less likely to be reported to the child protective system, and it is therefore the juvenile justice system that may be their last chance for any relevant AOD services before incarceration as an adult. Sadly, this group is also where the problems of substance abuse and family violence, to which we turn in the next section, most frequently overlap.

Family Violence, AOD Problems, and Child Welfare

The family violence problem overlaps child protective services caseloads in many of the same ways that AOD problems do. There are important differences between the two problems, but first we need to understand how family violence and AOD issues are similar:

> Many professionals traditionally viewed the presence of adult-on-adult family violence as a problem that was irrelevant to their goal of protecting the children, and therefore did not ask about it during screening, investigation, or assessment. As a result, effective child abuse interventions were often sabotaged by the ongoing occurrence and escalation of domestic violence over time, and the children remained in danger [Carter 1997].

If the words "domestic violence" and "family violence" were replaced with the words "AOD problems" in this selection, this quote would remain just as accurate. That underscores the extent to which both problems affect CWS caseloads and require changes in CWS practice to reduce the harm to children. Both problems are underemphasized in the typical CWS assessment, reflecting the limited training provided to CWS staff on the nature of the problems. Both problems undermine the effectiveness of child abuse interventions. For example, parent education courses may ignore the two problems in their curricula. Family preservation programs undermine efforts to address family violence and AOD problems if they screen out these parents (as some have acknowledged in a recent assessment of child abuse treatment outcomes in California) [Rosenbaum et al. 1997].

In addition to families in the CWS system, family violence and substance abuse also coexist in a significant number of other families. Both battered women and batterers are significantly affected by AOD use; several studies have found that more than 40% of homeless, lower-income women report both physical abuse and AOD abuse [Bassuk et al. 1986]. In a study of domestic assault incidents in Tennessee, 94% of the assailants and 43% of the victims had used alcohol and/ or other drugs in the six hours prior to the assault [Bookoff 1996]. A 1997 Treatment Improvement Protocol issued by the Center for Substance Abuse Treatment, titled *Substance Abuse Treatment and Domestic Violence,* included persuasive evidence that linked these two problems, and concluded that "failure to address domestic violence issues interferes with treatment effectiveness and contributes to relapse" [Fazzone et al. 1991].

Similarities Between Responses to Family Violence and AOD Problems

In response to these problems, similar proposals for reform have been developed by providers and advocates in both areas. These include strengthened training, revised assessment and screening protocols, access to experts in the specific fields of family violence and AOD, collaborative links to other agencies addressing problems of families in the CWS system, stronger links to community-based organizations and informal supports, and changes in court procedures and legal requirements. A review of Table 2 on models of linking CWS and AOD activities (on page 28) shows the similarities in approaches with the linkages being forged with family violence practitioners.

As is the case for AOD problems, the issue of assessment has special significance in addressing family violence, since routine assessment practices do not seek information on family violence in sufficient depth to ensure that this condition is tracked over time to determine its impact on the family. Several articles on family violence and its impact on families have recommended more thorough assessment practices, but without taking into account the "layering" effect discussed previously, in which each problem is the focus of another, entirely separate assessment. This problem of layered assessments also complicates making separate AOD assessments on top of current risk assessment procedures. An issue of added importance in assessing family violence problems is the need to conduct separate interviews with the victims of family violence, apart from the perpetrators of violence and their children.

Training is also an area of reform addressed by advocates for more attention to both AOD and family violence, with the models for AOD-CWS training described above as prime examples. Within the family violence field, training curricula have been developed by the Family Violence Prevention Fund and the University of Iowa for use in training CWS staff, as well as other human service intake workers, in several states and communities.*

In both areas, community norms are an important factor. On the one hand, there is still acceptance of family violence and substance abuse as "normal" behavior that is often viewed by law enforcement staff as a private matter within the family. However, the community can also serve as an important source of pressure on parents whose behavior endangers their children, as well as a source of support for parents who want help. Reforms aimed at law enforcement personnel and court staff have been undertaken as a means of improving the responses of both sets of critical agencies.

Specific language in the welfare reform legislation refers to family violence, and with the substantial overlap between AOD use and family violence, policy makers should carefully review the extent to which these two problems affect an overlapping group of both TANF and CWS clients.

Differences Between Responses to Family Violence and AOD Problems

In family violence situations, there are usually a clear perpetrator and a clear victim, as opposed to AOD problems in the CWS system,

---

* The Family Violence Prevention Fund, Esta Soler, Executive Director. 383 Rhode Island Street, Suite 304, San Francisco, CA 94103; 415/252-8900.

where the parents are abusing alcohol and/or other drugs or are chemically dependent in a way that affects their parenting. This difference in perspective regarding the target of intervention leads to a different focus for treatment and prevention. In the family violence situation, the batterer is the focus of treatment efforts and the victim is the focus for supportive services and advocacy. In the CWS system, the effects on children are the focus, but in the AOD system, the focus is on the AOD user.

Abuse is the typical problem for family violence victims in the CWS system, while neglect is a much more common problem for families affected by AOD (although some studies have found that alcohol abuse is correlated with physical abuse and illicit drug use is correlated with neglect) [Wilson 1996].

Sanctions are viewed differently in the two systems, with family violence agencies seeking heavier sanctions against perpetrators and AOD systems using sanctions to reinforce the behavior sought in improved parenting. Family violence personnel typically favor noncoercive intervention for victims and sanctions applied to perpetrators, with some important exceptions when children are endangered. AOD systems use both coercive and noncoercive treatment, since research shows little difference in the ultimate outcomes.

Working with Family Violence Prevention and Treatment Agencies

Unfortunately, these differences and the traditional tendency of the human service systems to take a categorical approach to all problems have meant that the majority of literature and training materials addressing AOD or family violence has almost completely ignored the other issue. As a 1994 review of child abuse and substance abuse stated:

> Experts have been identified in chemical dependency, child abuse, and violence, but cross-fertilization in these highly correlated fields seldom occurs [Blau et al. 1994].

There are important recent exceptions, however. Discussions sponsored by the Clark Foundation, both under the auspices of its Community Partnerships initiative and in an earlier Executive Session on the future of the CWS system convened by the John F. Kennedy School of Government at Harvard University from 1994 to 1997, have begun to frame the issues of the overlap more explicitly. Materials developed by Susan Schechter of the University of Iowa have proposed treatment programs that address both family violence and AOD problems of batterers [Schechter 1997]. But much remains to be done in this area.

Important organizational issues are also raised by the attempt to create new units that address family violence and AOD problems in the CWS system. Establishing a unit specifically to deal with family violence issues is an appropriate recommendation, although establishing a similar unit for AOD issues—and for child sexual abuse, mental health, and TANF liaison—is also appropriate. But a significant problem with forming a new unit is that it sometimes enables an organization to isolate an innovation and keep it away from the mainstream of the organization. The larger challenge may be *infusing the concepts* of sensitivity to both family violence and AOD problems throughout the organization. Recently, San Diego County, California, reorganized its health and human services agency to include an AOD focus in each of the new operating units, rather than in a separate, more isolated AOD unit. Massachusetts has used a separate unit to pilot interdisciplinary teams that include family violence expertise as well as other disciplines relevant to CWS. Service providers may not always welcome the infusion approach, as opposed to having their own identifiable unit. But at the very least, the trade-off between a new entity and the infusion approach should be addressed explicitly.

Finally, it is critical that efforts to improve the child welfare system's handling of both AOD problems and family violence devote adequate attention to documenting that such efforts will succeed in improving outcomes for children and families. As Aron and Olson note,

> It may be worthwhile to develop methods to justify these resources, such as documenting the number of families in need, tracking these families over time, and observing if they are more likely to reenter the child welfare system or use more

expensive services because of unaddressed domestic violence concerns [Aron & Olson 1997].

The same questions apply to AOD-targeted reforms, in which changes in clients, workers, and systems should all be the focus of serious evaluation designed to make the case for such reforms based on results, not just good intentions. These discussions about outcomes will get to the heart of some of the important philosophical differences in perspectives, including the issue of whether removal of children (and parents) from the home is an indicator of success or failure. In a serious discussion of outcomes across the boundaries of the fields of AOD, CWS, and family violence, the measures of success must be defined in ways that are clear to all three groups, while allowing flexibility for different perspectives on the needs of children and families (see Table 13).

The Link to Mental Health

Parents with substance abuse problems frequently have a variety of health and mental health complications. The increasingly common label "behavioral health" is usually intended to include mental health and substance abuse problems in the same broad category, suggesting the close connections between the two sets of conditions. In the total population, diagnosable mental health and substance abuse disorders are projected to affect 28% of the population; 22% of the population has a mental disorder, with anxiety (12.6%) and depression and other affective disorders (9.5%) the major categories. Substance abuse disorders are found in 9.5% of the population; thus, about 3.5% of the population has both mental health *and* substance abuse disorders [Goodwin et al. 1997]. A particular disorder among substance-abusing women with children who are victims of family violence is posttraumatic stress disorder, as documented by a wide array of studies and the experience of women's centers [Dansky et al. 1997].

These findings are a powerful reinforcement of the premise of this guidebook that the lines between these often-overlapping conditions, however categorically they may be defined at entry to the sepa-

Table 13. Similarities and Differences in Approaches to Family Violence and AOD Problems

	Family Violence	AOD
Values	Public attitudes tend to polarize Gender bias affects values Victim and perpetrator seen differently Perpetrator's personal responsibility is central to better outcomes Children seen as victimized	Public attitudes tend to polarize AOD stigma affects values Addict seen as focus of treatment Addict's motivation is critical factor in better outcomes Children rarely the focus of treatment (except in perinatal programs)
Screening Brief questions to trigger in-depth assessment	3-5 threshold questions widely accepted	Screening instruments widely accepted in AOD, but most often used in CWS are biological markers (testing)
Assessment	Five questions form core of assessment process Assessment needs to continue throughout contact with case; risk continues	Moves beyond AOD use to functioning in key life areas: health, crime, employment, psychological status, social/family relationships
Perspectives on Treatment	Wide skepticism about treatment outcomes among perpetrators Victim is not "treated," but provided advocacy/services Family needs protection from perpetrator	Growing reliance on treatment if well matched to client Addict is focus of treatment Treatment outcomes are better with family support, employment, and persons without mental illness
Training	Curriculum exists for inservice training	Curriculum exists for inservice training
Outcomes	Not widely used to assess services effectiveness yet	Growing use, especially in treatment outcomes in managed care settings
Budgets	Focus is upon categorical funding	Moving from categorical AOD-only funding to some wraparound and other sources
Advocacy Strategies	Close ties among national organizations	Rivalries sometimes exist among different modalities and constituencies
Links to CPS	Increasing linkages Mother sometimes seen as cause of "failure to protect" children at risk	Increasing linkages but CPS is primary actor to make linkage at this point Mother who has AOD problem is a risk factor and must satisfy court and fulfill service plan

rate systems, are far less distinct than current practice suggests. For those women who are multiply affected by poverty, mental illness, family violence, and AOD abuse, their own lives are often ample evidence that separate systems cannot deal with interpellated problems; when the focus shifts to the lives of their children, who have often witnessed the violence and other disruptive episodes that accompany these conditions, the impact can be even greater in long-term effects.

There have been several recent assessments of the connections between AOD problems and mental health, including a review of behavioral health and other barriers to welfare-to-work transitions produced by Olson and Pavetti at the Urban Institute in 1996; a Treatment Improvement Protocol issued by the Center for Substance Abuse Treatment, titled *Assessment and Treatment of Patients with Coexisting Mental Illness and Alcohol and Other Drug Abuse;* and the California-specific guidebook *The Impact of Behavioral Health on Employability of Public Assistance Recipients,* issued by the California Institute for Mental Health [Pavetti et al. 1996]. While none of these places a spotlight on child welfare issues, their focus on the TANF population enables some generalizations about the CWS population as well.

Again, assessment issues are important in developing responses to mental health problems within the child welfare and AOD-abusing population. The standard instruments used for initial screening for mental heath problems are unique to the mental health field, as are those in substance abuse, CPS risk assessment, and family violence. So some parents in the TANF system may be screened five separate times for job readiness, parenting skills, mental health, substance abuse, and family violence.

As one means of responding to this problem, the CSAT protocol recommends use of simple screening techniques to detect the presence of psychiatric disorders, including both a CAGE-type tool for AOD problems and a brief mental status exam for mental disorders. The protocol recommends that "all frontline AOD and mental health staff receive detailed training in the use of a mental status exam and AOD screening tests" [Ries 1994].

Other issues raised by the connection between mental health, substance abuse, and child welfare are the extent to which Medicaid funds reimburse states and localities for mental health treatment, the availability of needed medications for parents with diagnosed disorders, the mix of different skills and training needed in treating substance-abusing and mentally ill clients, and the optimum organizational configuration of a set of services and supports that respond to the problems of clients with these overlapping conditions.

With regard to the last issue, several sources note that mental health and AOD treatment are often combined in state agencies, either in a single behavioral health unit as part of a health department or in a single "superagency" that includes mental health and AOD treatment issues (and sometimes even child welfare) under an overhead agency. One recommendation that emerges from this configuration is for common identifiers in data collection across AOD abuse and mental health treatment. This would obviously enable data matching of those clients with dual disorders with far greater accuracy than is usually possible in separate agencies with separate data bases.

Confidentiality Issues in Working with Other Systems

As CWS and AOD agencies reach out to work with agencies and providers in other systems, the issue of client confidentiality becomes a concern. Though both CWS and AOD agencies must adhere to confidentiality laws, regulations governing the disclosure of AOD treatment information are much more restrictive. Federal law (42 U.S.C. § 290dd-2) and its accompanying regulations (42 CFR Part 2) require federally assisted alcohol or drug programs to strictly maintain the confidentiality of client records. Furthermore, many states have their own confidentiality laws and regulations that also must be followed [Lopez 1994]. An excellent source in dealing with these issues is the publication *Glass Walls,* issued by the Youth Law Center in San Francisco [Soler et al. 1993].

No one disputes that these privacy laws are important to encourage people to seek treatment and protect the release of information that may be adversely used in their professional and personal lives. Yet, such laws and regulations also compound the distrust and lack of communication among the many professionals working with substance-abusing parents and their children. Despite 1986 federal regulatory changes intended to enable substance abuse programs to generate state-mandated child abuse reports, a treatment agency must still protect patient records from subsequent disclosures and not permit them to be used in child abuse proceedings against the patient—unless the patient consents or a court order is issued.

Under specific conditions, sharing of client treatment information is acceptable—for instance, if information is needed within a program to provide substance abuse services to the patient, or if a patient authorizes disclosure by signing a valid consent form. Increasingly, child welfare service agencies that are working as part of interagency collaboratives or case management teams are turning to the use of informed consent forms with their clients. Some providers work out informal agreements that operate as trust builds across agency lines. It should also be noted that sometimes what an agency needs most from another agency are not specific names of clients, but overall totals for purposes of data matching to assess the extent of overlapping—which does not violate anyone's confidentiality. In short, familiarity with confidentiality laws and regulations is essential to any agency working with families requiring substance abuse treatment and prevention.

References

Aron, L. Y., & Olson, K. K. (1997). Efforts by child welfare agencies to address domestic violence. *Public Welfare, 55*(3).

Bassuk, E. L., Rubin, L., & Lauriat, A. (1986). Characteristics of sheltered homeless families. *American Journal of Public Health, 76,* 1097-1101.

Blau, G. M., Whewell, M. C., Gullota, T. P., & Bloom, M. (1994). The prevention and treatment of child abuse in households of substance abusers: A research demonstration progress report. *Child Welfare, 73* (1), 83-94.

Brookoff, D. (1996). *Drug use and domestic violence.* National Institute of Justice Research in Progress Seminar Series. Washington, DC: National Criminal Justice Reference Service.

Bruner, C., & Parachini, L. (1997). *Building community.* Washington, DC: Institute for Educational Leadership.

Carter, J. (1997). *Improving child welfare response to domestic violence: Considerations for policy and practice.* San Francisco, CA: Family Violence Prevention Fund.

Child welfare and juvenile justice must collaborate, leaders say. (1997). *Child Protection Report*, 23(22). Silver Spring, MD: Business Publishers.

Child Welfare League of America (1992). *Children at the front.* Washington, DC: Author.

Christian, S. (1997). *New directions for child protective services.* Denver, CO: National Conference of State Legislatures.

Dansky, B., Saladin, M., Coffey, S., & Brady, K. (1997). Use of self-report measures of crime-related posttraumatic stress disorder with substance use disordered patients. *Journal of Substance Abuse Treatment, 14*(5), 431-37.

Fazzone, P. A., Holton, J. K., & Reed, B. G. (1991). *Substance abuse treatment and domestic violence.* Rockville, MD: U.S. Department of Health and Human Services, Public Health Service, Substance Abuse and Mental Health Services Administration, Center for Substance Abuse Treatment. DHHS Publication No. (SMA) 97-3163. 5.

Goodwin, S. N., Geary, C., Meisel, J., & Chandler, D. (1997). *The impact of behavioral health on employability of public assistance recipients: A technical assistance guide to the current state of knowledge.* Sacramento, CA: California Institute for Mental Heath.

Kelley, B. T., Thornberry, T. P., & Smith, C. A. (1997). In the wake of child maltreatment. *OJJDP Juvenile Justice Bulletin.* Washington, DC: U.S. Department of Justice, Office of Justice Programs, Office of Juvenile Justice and Delinquency Prevention.

Lopez, F. (1994). *Confidentiality of patient records for alcohol and other drug treatment,* Rockville, MD: U.S. Department of Health and Human Services, Public Health Service, Substance Abuse and Mental Health Services Administration, Center for Substance Abuse Treatment.

Morgan, L., & Gutterman, F. (1995). *Sacramento County division of family preservation and child protection preliminary report.* Washington, DC: Child Welfare League of America and National Center for Excellence in Child Welfare.

McPhail, M. W., & West, B. M. (Panel co-chairs). (1995). *Combining alcohol and other drug treatment with diversion for juveniles in the justice system.* Washington, DC: Center for Substance Abuse Treatment.

Pavetti, L., Olsen, K., Pindus, N., Pernas, M., & Isaacs, J. (1996). *Designing welfare-to-work programs for families facing personal or family challenges: Lessons from the field.* Washington, DC: The Urban Institute.

Pear, R. (January 21, 1998). Number on welfare dips below ten million. *The New York Times.*

Ries, R. (Panel chair). (1994). *Assessment and treatment of patients with coexisting mental illness and alcohol and other drug abuse.* Washington, DC: Center for Substance Abuse Treatment.

Rosenbaum, J., Robinson, G., & Gardner, S. L. (1997). *A feasibility analysis of the transition to outcomes-based evaluation for the Office of Criminal Justice Planning Projects funded by the Victims of Crime Act: Child abuse.* Fullerton, CA: California State University, Fullerton, Center for Collaboration for Children.

Schechter, S. (1997). *Creating safety for women and children.* A paper prepared for the meeting, "Developing a Community Partnership for Family Safety." New York: Edna McConnell Clark Foundation.

Sherman, L. W., Gottfredson, D., MacKenzie, D., Eck, J., Reuter, P., & Bushway, S. (1997). *Preventing crimes: What works, what doesn't, what's promising.* Washington, DC: National Institute of Justice.

Soler, M., Shotton, A., & Bell J. (1993). *Glass walls: Confidentiality provisions and interagency collaborations.* San Francisco, CA: Youth Law Center.

Wilson, J. B. (1996). *Abused and neglected children: How many? How serious the maltreatment? What share could be reached only through corrective intervention?* Cambridge, MA: Malcolm Weiner Center for Social Policy and Program in Criminal Justice Policy and Management, John F. Kennedy School of Government, Harvard University.

Young, N. K., & Gardner, S. L. (1997). *Bridge building: An action plan for state and county efforts to strengthen links between child welfare services and services for alcohol and other drug problems.* Irvine, CA: Children and Family Futures.

7

Building the Future: Recommendations

Some of the lessons gleaned from the model projects and from recent innovations are about the *external policy environment* of CWS-AOD linkages, such as the importance of community values and norms, the powerful impact of crisis and the media response to crisis, and the wide range of other initiatives going on outside the child welfare system that can influence it, such as welfare reform and community development efforts. But some of the lessons pertain to *internal*, agency-specific issues that bear upon implementation of practices; these include the importance of the conduct of leaders, the development and provision of training, and the prime issue of assessment across and within systems.

Some of the recommendations made in this chapter focus on *policy changes*, such as the budgeting shifts needed to blend funds from both CWS and AOD systems. Other suggestions involve changes at the *practice level*, such as the nature of the actual forms to be used in assessment and the training needed to ensure a connection between new practice and the attitudes and competencies of existing staff. In Table 14, we set out recommendations according to the corresponding element of our policy framework and the related observations.

The First Steps: A Recommended Action Agenda

With these summary lessons in mind, using the six-part policy framework makes it possible to develop a set of action steps that should guide child welfare agencies as they move toward broader CWS-AOD links. Ten steps can be outlined that are critical:

- Make a comprehensive statement of values and principles that goes beyond "motherhood and apple pie" generali-

Table 14. Recommendations for Policy and Practice Changes

The Lessons/Policy Element	The Recommendations
Values Matter External crisis drives the values debate at times Diversity of communities; means one size won't fit all	Frame the values choices for community-wide discussion, but first assess where the areas of consensus and disagreement are deepest (Collaborative Values inventory) Develop marketing and public education approaches as part of innovation Understand the leverage potential of a crisis; market changes in noncrisis times Design approaches based on community-specific data on needs and values
Daily Practice Assessment as the common bond; staffing options	(See assessment recommendations on page xx) Weigh pros and cons of each staffing model
Outcomes and Information Systems Innovation and results-based accountability Feedback loops increase accountability & threaten workers	Make clear that results-based accountability needs a transitional period Negotiate fair measures as gradual outcomes
Training Take staff seriously as partners Mapping change: find the allies and the blockers Dealing with senior managers Leadership matters	Develop explicit line staff and senior manager consultation efforts Training reforms for line staff and senior managers
Budget Scope and scale of reform: reversion to categorical pilot projects Going from pilots to policy; the filters for choosing strategic pilots Fragmented financing in categorical, agency-specific patterns	Clarify boundaries and key partners, based on data and opportunities for collaboration Develop a theory of resources and a redirection agenda Expand blended funding waivers and permissive legislation Collect and update annual spending inventories
Service Delivery The overlap of AOD and CWS with TANF, family violence, and juvenile justice and mental health Which external agencies are key partners? Parallel reforms undermine or reinforce change	Negotiate specific interagency protocols and memoranda of understanding Monitor TANF impact and welfare reform evaluation as special concern area Data-driven partnerships; get the numbers on overlap Map initiatives in collaboration matrices

ties and that reflects careful consideration of important values issues, such as the following:

- The state/county/city policy on harm reduction;
- The community policy on working toward treatment on demand for all parents who are seeking help and complying with treatment requirements; and
- The community response to the debate about responses to pregnant mothers with AOD problems, ranging from punitive prosecution to encouraging these women to enter treatment without fear of legal action as long as they comply with treatment requirements.

- Develop a public education plan which explains the innovations that will bridge CWS-AOD agencies and which provides substantiation for the actual need for these services—cite data on the parents seeking help and children who will be affected.

- Consider use of the Collaborative Values Inventory (see Appendix A) with key stakeholder groups as a means of assessing consensus and disagreements on values and community norms.

- Review and upgrade local data on the problem as needed. This requires the following:

  - Estimating the prevalence of AOD problems among the different categories of families in the CWS system, as well as the prevalence of TANF and CWS families among current AOD client caseloads, using data matching, case reviews, sampling, and other tools;
  - Documenting the resources—both staff and contract services—devoted to providing AOD services to CWS parents;
  - Reviewing and upgrading the outcomes and indicators used to monitor the effectiveness of AOD treatment for CWS parents; and

- Developing a local "scorecard" of overall CWS-AOD conditions that could be monitored annually for community-wide signs of progress in addressing the overlapping populations.

- Review current assessment tools for their AOD content and the "layering" effect of different tools to develop blended approaches, with screening done by CWS staff and detailed, follow-on assessment done by AOD staff.

- Design organizational innovation and new staffing patterns based on detailed analysis of the pros and cons of each model as they relate to the specific community involved and the need to work effectively with other collaboratives and parallel initiatives.

- Develop a multiyear funding and staffing plan across agencies that reflects the prevalence (based on data from preceding steps) of AOD problems in caseloads for CWS, TANF, family violence agencies, juvenile justice systems, and mental health agencies. This plan should include the total allocations of AOD slots, if any, for each of these five overlapping population groups.

- Use results-based accountability principles to evaluate and fund provider agencies; accordingly, modify contracts to reflect results-based accountability, allowing for a gradual transition period to enable agencies to move toward results-based accountability with training and support as they do so.

- Review outcomes as they affect the capacity to redirect resources, in which the key question is: What outcomes would convince policymakers to expand pilot programs? Keep issues of scale visible and explicit by asking what percentage of community needs would be addressed by a proposed project.

- Develop a multiyear staff development plan. All Title IV-E funded training should be reviewed in depth to determine whether adequate AOD content is included in training provided during orientation of new employees, as well as "booster shot" training on an inservice basis and whether the training is likely to achieve new competencies sought. Court and law enforcement staff should be included in such training, as well as supervisors and departmental senior managers from both agencies.

Further Reflections on Training Models

If assessment is the key element that helps agencies respond more effectively to clients across the CWS and AOD systems, training is the ingredient that ensures that workers in both systems have the knowledge, skills, and attitudes needed to play such a role. But training is too often treated as a single injection, rather than an ongoing process that may require an occasional "booster shot."

It is critical to involve both line staff and their supervisors in training. As the Sacramento AODTI project team observes:

> The staff realized late in the process that an informational seminar should have been offered for mid-managers and supervisors first. They felt that the project was imposed on them. Although a management seminar was subsequently provided, some residual impact continues to affect change efforts. Significant time must be spent nurturing "buy-in" among supervisors and managers before attempting a system shift with line staff [Klopp 1997].

A sustained dialogue among county-level CWS and AOD officials in California produced a set of training agendas in which both "sides" specified what they thought the other needed to know, which are described in Table 15.

Again, training by itself rarely changes practice. But training as part of the bridge across systems can help agencies become clearer about what they are missing and where they can get it.

Table 15. Proposed Training Agendas

Training Content for CWS Staff	Training Content for AOD Staff
AOD issues: use, abuse, and dependence	How the child welfare system works
How to identify and intervene with AOD dependence	Trends in local CWS and out-of-home care
Treatment modalities and effectiveness—what providers do and their capacity What local resources exist and how they differ	Local resources in the child welfare system: parenting education, shelters, foster homes
AOD as a family disease; the dynamics of AOD-abusing families; impact on parenting	AOD as a family disease; the dynamics of AOD-abusing families; impact on parenting
Confidentiality laws	Confidentiality laws
Matching level of functioning to levels of care	Resources available for family-oriented interventions and family support/aftercare
The special needs of women and fathers/significant others	Developmental impact of AOD use—both prenatal and environmental—on children
The language used in AOD and other systems	The language used in child welfare and other systems
The "four clocks"—different timetables in the other systems	The "four clocks"—different timetables in the other systems

Working with Other Systems: A Review of Recommendations

As discussed in Chapter 6, strengthening CWS-AOD connections is not enough, given the extent to which these clients need other services provided by agencies beyond either child welfare or AOD systems. The most important of these connections are with the TANF system, the juvenile justice system, the agencies that address family violence, and the mental health system.

In working with the TANF population, the two priorities for action must be (1) to document the overlap between the two populations and (2) to seek an allocation of the maximum amount of TANF funding for the CWS/TANF population that now overlaps—or that might overlap in the future. While negotiating these allocations and referral relationships, CWS and TANF units must also work with other agencies in defining the outcomes that will be used to evaluate the effectiveness of welfare reform, especially its projected impact on child abuse and neglect.

For the juvenile justice population, several recent assessments have set out the arguments about "what works." Two critical recommendations emerge: (1) increase the focus on services for children, especially for the middle group of 5- to 12-year-olds; and (2) develop family-focused interventions targeting younger children once they are identified as being at risk as a result of their first contacts with the juvenile justice system and following their identification in the child welfare system.

With respect to family violence, the materials presented in Chapter 6 describe the necessary kinds of assessment, training, and AOD-specific services. The similarities and differences between the two systems as they affect daily practice need to be reviewed in staff training. Again assessment is critical, since separate AOD and family violence assessments are likely to lead to clients and workers both reacting negatively to the duplication and time costs resulting from "layered assessment."

In the mental health system, what is needed is, again, documenting the local overlaps in caseloads. Then, CWS workers must cooperate with mental health agencies to ensure that AOD treatment and mental health services are provided in a complementary way by therapists and counselors familiar with clients with dual diagnoses. Difficult issues of funding streams, time in treatment, and the overlap with TANF clients all challenge CWS and AOD agencies as they try to build their own bridges to each other, while addressing the very real problems of those clients they share who also have serious mental health problems. The priority recommendation for a CWS-AOD-based effort to respond to mental health problems is to document both client needs and available resources in the community.

CASE STUDY Sacramento County Update. The AODTI remains a vital initiative that is still much more than a training initiative and that addresses several other facets of the CWS-AOD connection. In recent months (as of March 1998) the Sacramento project has moved into a more neighborhood-specific approach, working with two neighborhood service centers where there is a multidisciplinary team and active concern for the AOD agenda. In addition, the commitment to the training portion of the AODTI remains so strong that virtually all of the more than 170 new hires in the Department of Health and Human Services have gone through Level I training. A new "gatekeeper" role has been established in the Bureau of Alcohol and Drug Programs for the purpose of maintaining a current inventory on all treatment capacity throughout the AOD system, which enables all human service workers to contact one staff person responsible for providing accurate information about community providers and available slots. The gatekeeper will also reinforce priority slots for CWS clients. The implementation of welfare reform in the county has adopted several of the key features of the AODTI. Finally, the county has been selected as one of six counties in the state in which new risk assessment tools will be developed, although the degree of emphasis upon AOD issues within those instruments is yet to be determined.

Expanded Funding Versus Improved Systems: Different Kinds of Capacity

It is obvious that for some of the changes proposed in this document, more funding will be needed to increase the number of persons who can be treated and to reduce caseloads to a level where these innovations can be effective. With more than 50,000 specifically identifiable persons in state waiting lists at present, and an estimated 1 million more in need of treatment, compared with the 1.8 million total slots in current publicly funded treatment programs, there remains a fundamental resources question [NASADAD 1997].

Yet expansion of funding for the current fragmented, nonaccountable system, as desperately as these services may be needed, will be less effective than working *at the same time* to improve the capacity of both CWS and AOD systems to utilize new funding in a newly connected system. As stated in Chapter 4, we believe that improved assessment is a primary prerequisite for system change, without which more funding for today's systems will simply create larger, but still disconnected systems. It is the balance between the system changes and the resource changes that is crucial; we should neither overwhelm today's fragmented systems with new resources nor try to improve capacity in a vacuum while ignoring how much new treatment resources are needed.

As important as they are, greatly improved assessment procedures and staff who are well-trained in their use and motivated to use them *cannot compensate for insufficient capacity and inadequate resources.* Assessment is not treatment. With waiting lists as lengthy as they are today—especially for the family-oriented programs needed for the clients who overlap the CWS-AOD systems—the resources agenda and the capacity-strengthening agenda must go hand in hand.

"Capacity," therefore, means two different things. Expanded capacity needed for implementation of TANF, for example, means that in some states millions of dollars of new funding for support services, including some funds set aside by state policy for AOD treatment, is now moving toward treatment providers whose ability to serve TANF clients has not yet changed and whose beds and treatment slots may not be readily expandable. That is the first kind of capacity: the sheer ability to provide services to more people.

But the second kind of capacity is what this report is about—the ability to work across the CWS and AOD systems (as well as the TANF, juvenile justice, family violence, and mental health systems). We strongly assert that those agencies that are making efforts to become more family-focused, community-based, and accountable for results are those whose treatment slots should be increased first—because they are working on both kinds of capacity improvements.

Once these critical prerequisites are in place, the funding itself must be as broad as the strategies that seek to combine CWS and AOD practice. Funding must be multiagency and multiyear in nature, rather than relying upon a single line item to support CWS-AOD links.

To support these needs with a new categorical line item, in fact, would be a major step backward, since it would divert efforts to blend existing funding toward another round of grant chasing and RFPs for much smaller amounts of money.

Sources that should be included in a serious multiyear, multisource funding strategy are listed below:

- Medicaid;

- The new Child Health Improvement Program legislation;

- Title IV child welfare funds (under federal waivers as appropriate);

- TANF support services—both those funded directly to states and those funded through Private Industry Councils and Family Preservation and Support funds;

- State-channeled formula and project grants under the Substance Abuse Prevention and Treatment Block Grant;

- Discretionary funding under both the Center for Substance Abuse Prevention (CSAP) and CSAT, where community-wide collaboratives are seriously engaged in strengthening CWS-AOD linkages;

- Safe and Drug Free schools; and

- Appropriate state line-item funding available for specific target groups or program modalities, such as adolescent treatment or home visiting linked to AOD services.

Action Needed at the Federal Level

For the most part, this report has focused on action at the community level, with some state policy changes specified. But the previous section makes clear that the federal government remains a critical player in several areas:

- Federal budget policy in the area of welfare reform, the implementation of the new Adoption and Safe Families Act governing child welfare, the use of new Title XXI funds in the Child Health Insurance Program, and the future of the Substance Abuse Prevention and Treatment Block Grant all make up part of the financing landscape for CWS-AOD connections, determining the feasibility of blended funding and several of the other recommendations in this report. This includes the authority given to DHHS to grant up to 10 state waivers for child welfare demonstration projects.

- The terms of federal funding, especially funding conditions that require or encourage outcome data as part of reporting or evaluation, can provide major incentives for an accelerated move toward results-based accountability and capacity building among both CWS and AOD agencies.

- Federal research and demonstration programs, notably the currently expiring perinatal grants for treatment programs for pregnant and parenting mothers, have supported several of the models discussed in this report. These programs include some of the best models of CWS-AOD practice, and they should receive federal technical assistance in blended funding that combines CWS, AOD, and other relevant funding streams.

- Federal data collection activities through the several data sets maintained by the various agencies that address child welfare and AOD treatment issues determine a great deal of the available national data and whether they cover children and families in the AOD system or AOD issues in the CWS agencies.

The enactment of the Adoption and Safe Families Act in 1997 affords a unique opportunity to the federal agencies that affect the problems of CWS-AOD linkages. Section 405 of that Act requires the Secretary of Health and Human Services to work with both the Substance Abuse and Mental Health Services Administration and the Administration for Children and Families in preparing, in the words of the legislation:

> ... a report which describes the extent and scope of the problem of substance abuse in the child welfare population, the types of services provided to such population, and the outcomes resulting from the provision of such services to such population. That report shall include recommendations for any legislation that may be needed to improve coordination in providing such services to such population.

This reporting requirement is an opportunity for federal agencies and their interested partners to frame all these issues at a higher level of visibility and to set forth a federal agenda that is proactive and built on the best practices at state and community levels. The federal agencies could themselves model CWS-AOD linkages in developing and disseminating to selected states and communities the authority to blend several types of federal resources. Such funding, which some have called "bottom-up block grants," would enable states or communities to blend portions of categorical funding, as long as those funds are aimed at the purposes of the ASFA legislation and use outcome measures to assess annual progress. (A separate section of the legislation, Section 203(a), calls for further federal attention to CWS outcome measures.) In its work with several states and communities over the past four years, the National Performance Review (NPR) initiative has made efforts at repackaging federal grants and technical assistance. Linking the NPR with the new legislation would raise the priority given to the CWS-AOD agenda within DHHS and other federal departments.

A special mention should also be made of the capacity and responsibility of the federal government to improve data collection. The

Office of National Drug Control Policy, SAMHSA, and the National Institute on Drug Abuse have begun to address some of the weaknesses in current federal surveys and other data collection efforts that hinder accurate estimation of the prevalence of CWS-AOD problems. This is an opportunity to ensure that a particular focus on children is included in each of the surveillance and outcome monitoring systems maintained by the federal and state governments. We recommend wider collection within AOD information systems of data on the children of substance-abusing parents.

Conclusion

As stated previously, an obvious paradox in child welfare services is that working with service systems beyond the traditional parameters of child welfare has become the only hope for success in achieving the goals of the child welfare system. That paradox—that success for many of the children and families *in* the child welfare system can only come from working with services and supports from *outside* CWS—is at the heart of our recommendations for continuing the efforts to strengthen the links between CWS and AOD services. The success of those efforts will affect millions of families and their children, and the potential savings in resources will more than repay the investment needed.

But recognizing the importance of external players does not reduce the accountability of the child welfare system for its own actions. Nor does it reduce in any way the demands of leadership that the child welfare system itself must provide in rallying external resources. Seven years ago, the CWLA Commission on Chemical Dependency and Child Welfare concluded its report, *Children at the Front,* with this call to action:

> Child welfare and other health and human service agencies must become actively involved in our nation's efforts to prevent alcohol and drug problems and to better address problems when prevention efforts fail....The Commission challenges the policies and practices of current national and state

efforts and the policies and practices of many child and family agencies [CWLA 1992].

We must remain true to that challenge and work on both practice and policy in the child welfare system, as the 1992 report proposed. We must keep in view the lessons drawn from the best projects described in this report and the knowledge of the terrible losses we will suffer if another generation of children affected by alcohol and other drugs is left without the help they need. This is not optional work to be done after the basic operational tasks of child welfare agencies are finished; it *is* the basic mission of the child welfare system as it responds to the needs of millions of children and their parents.

References

Child Welfare League of America (1992). *Children at the front: A different view of the war on alcohol and drugs.* Washington, DC: Author.

Kloop, G. H. (1997, Fall). Reshaping alcohol and other drug services: Sacramento County Department of Health and Human Services Alcohol and Other Drug Treatment Initiative. *Georgia Academy Journal,* 12-14.

National Association of State Alcohol and Drug Abuse Directors [NASADAD]. (1997). *Estimated number of individuals needing treatment.* Washington, DC: Author.

Appendix A
Collaborative Values Inventory

Explanation: Many collaboratives begin their work without much discussion in depth of what their members agree upon—or what they don't agree upon as well. This questionnaire can serve as a neutral, anonymous way of assessing how much a group shares ideas about the values that underlie their work. It can bring to the surface issues that may not be raised if the collaborative begins its discussion with programs and grant proposals, rather than with what its members really value in doing their work. To know that a group may have strong disagreements about some of the most basic assumptions about their community and its needs and resources may help the group clarify later disagreements about less important issues that are really about these more important underlying values.

Each question should be administered anonymously to a group, using a Likert 1-7 scale for each.

1. Dealing with the problems caused by alcohol and other drugs would improve the lives of a significant number of children, families, and others in need in our community.

2. Dealing with the problems caused by alcohol and other drugs should be one of the highest priorities for funding services in our community.

3. People who abuse alcohol and other drugs should be held fully responsible for their own actions.

4. There is no way that a parent who *abuses* alcohol or other drugs can be an effective parent.

5. There is no way that a parent who *uses* alcohol or other drugs can be an effective parent.

6. There is no way that a parent who is chemically depen-
    dent on alcohol or other drugs can be an effective parent.

7. In assessing the effects of the use of alcohol and other drugs,
    the standard we should use for deciding when to remove
    children from their parents is whether the parents are fully
    abstaining from use of alcohol or other drugs.

8. In assessing the effects of the use of alcohol and other drugs,
    the standard we should use for deciding when to remove
    children from their parents is whether the parents are com-
    petently parenting and whether their children are safe.

9. We have enough money in the systems that respond to the
    problems of alcohol and other drugs today; what we need
    is more effective programs using the funding we already
    have.

10. We should fund programs that serve children and families
    based on their results, not based on the number of people
    they serve, as we often do at present.

11. We should fund programs that treat parents for their abuse
    of alcohol and other drugs based on their results, not based
    on the number of people they serve, as we often do at
    present.

12. If we funded programs based on results, some programs
    would lose some or all of their funding.

13. The agencies in our community do a good job of involving
    people from the community in planning and evaluating
    programs that serve families and respond to the problems
    of substance abuse.

14. Changing the system so that more services were delivered closer to the neighborhoods and community level would improve the effectiveness of services.

15. Changing the system to allow more services to be delivered by for-profit agencies would improve the effectiveness of services.

16. Changing the system to require that all clients, regardless of income, who receive services should make some kind of payment for the services with donated time, services, or cash would improve the effectiveness of services.

17. If agencies delivering services to children and families would work more closely together when they are serving the same families, the effectiveness of services would improve.

18. The most important causes of the problems of children and families cannot be addressed by government; they need to be addressed within the family and by such nongovernmental organizations as churches, neighborhood organizations, and self-help groups.

19. The problems caused by use of tobacco by youth are largely unrelated to the problems caused by the use of alcohol and other drugs by youth.

20. A neighborhood's residents should have the right to decide how many liquor stores should be allowed in their neighborhood.

21. The messages that youth receive from the media, TV, music, etc. are a big part of the problem of abuse of alcohol and other drugs by youth.

22. The price of alcohol and tobacco should be increased to a point where it pays for the damage caused in the community by use and abuse of these legal drugs.

23. The most important causes of problems affecting children, families, and others in need in our community are [circle only three]:

a lack of self-discipline
a loss of family values
racism
drug abuse
mental illness
domestic violence
alcoholism
poverty
economic changes that have eliminated good jobs
low intelligence
inadequate support for low-income families who work
lack of skills needed to keep a good job
the harm done by government programs
illegal immigration
the level of violence tolerated by the community
the drug business
incompetent parenting
too few law enforcement personnel
fragmented systems of service delivery
deteriorating public schools
the way the welfare program works
children born and raised in single-parent homes
a lack of business involvement in solutions
too few jails and prisons
illiteracy
child abuse
an overemphasis upon consumer values
media concentration on negatives
other_____

Appendix B
A Dialogue on Practice and Policy

The group had been meeting for four months, following a widely publicized death of a child in the care of the child welfare system, who was severely beaten, and later died, at the hands of a stepfather who was drunk at the time. The group consisted of senior staff from the local child welfare agency, the local substance abuse agency, city and county governments, a treatment center operator, the local high school, and several members of the community.

"Are we ready to make some decisions today on some projects that will show the community that we're serious?" asked the group's co-chair, the deputy director of the child welfare agency.

"I hope so," said the other co-chair, a community leader who was pastor of a large church in the neighborhood where the child had lived. "It's about time we got some visible projects going."

The regional substance abuse agency director spoke up. "We've come up with a great list of projects—now we need to launch some. We've taken long enough talking about the problem."

A local businessman from the neighborhood looked worried. "I agree we've made a lot of progress. But I'm not sure about these projects. Are they really going to help? I thought this group was going to be about something more than a few new projects on top of all the projects we already have going on in this neighborhood. Will a few new projects really help save the children and families we are concerned about?"

The vice-principal of the local high school joined in, saying, "That bothers me, too. The United Way has a list of more than 30 parent education programs already providing services in this city. Setting up number 31 may not make much difference if we can't tell whether any of the ones already out there are helping parents who want to deal with their drug and drinking problems."

The minister asked, "Whatever happened to that neighborhood inventory that we were going to do? How much are we spending now for treatment services to people from this neighborhood?"

A young budget analyst from the city government spoke up. "I'm glad you asked. We just finished our first draft last week, and we were surprised to find out that the city, county, school district, and state are spending a total of $3.5 million a year on prevention and treatment services targeted directly on this area."

"$3.5 million!" exclaimed the minister. "Where is it?"

The city staffer continued, "That counts the school prevention programs for kids, the police department's prevention programs aimed at drugs and gangs, police patrol time related to drugs and alcohol, treatment for parents and others who gave this neighborhood as their address, the methadone maintenance program, and your area's share of the hospital clinic that runs day treatment programs for this whole side of the city. If you count the treatment services for inmates originally from this neighborhood, the number gets even higher. And of course that doesn't count all the voluntary self-help programs that aren't funded by government. There are a lot of churches that provide help to programs like that, and none of that is in the budget."

"Could we get that budget every year, so it's updated and we can see what happens to those programs from year to year instead of just getting it once?" asked the vice-principal.

The city staffer replied, "I can't speak for the elected folks, but if a majority of the people on a diverse group like this asked the city council and the county commissioners for it, I'll bet it would be made a staff priority. That's what has happened in some other cities around the country that have developed children's budgets and prevention budgets that they update every year."

The vice-principal said, "Let's go back to talking about what we're going to do. Maybe we should ask how these new projects on the list we've developed would affect any of that spending that is already there—and who should get priority treatment in these programs. Do we know who benefits from the old treatment programs?"

"We have some of that, but it would take some more work to break out just who the clients really are," said the treatment program director.

"But how do we measure whether things are getting better in this area?" asked the businessman.

The child welfare deputy director answered. "We have begun to collect some neighborhood indicators that would measure some of this. We want to measure both successes—like kids served by the prevention programs and people successfully completing treatment— and things that are problems, like new liquor outlets, DUI arrests, arrests for drug sales and possession, and domestic violence incidents reported by the police that involve drugs or drinking."

Looking troubled, the vice-principal spoke up. "Wait a minute. Why would kids in programs be counted as a positive if the programs don't work? How do we know which programs work?"

The city staff assistant said "Good question. We really don't, because most of these programs are funded based on their numbers or the need in the area, not the results they achieve."

"The good news is that the state has begin to rewrite its contracts so that funding is based on results achieved, but they are going to take three years to make the transition from intake-based funding to results-based funding," said the regional treatment program supervisor.

"So what do we do in the meantime?" asked the minister.

The vice-principal spoke up. "Well, what if we funded these new projects based on the willingness of the groups we fund to keep track of their results, not just how many people they see? We could help them with some training for their staff and boards. I've always wanted to know what we're getting out of all the money we put into school-based prevention."

The businessman said, "That makes sense. But once we decide what programs we want, how do we decide who gets them? Is it just first come, first served? Don't we need a study to find out how many of the parents in trouble with CPS have drug and alcohol problems and who they are?"

"We all know it's 70 to 80% of the caseload," said the child welfare deputy director wearily. "We don't need any more studies to tell us that."

The businessman wasn't persuaded. "But wait a minute—I've heard you say that several times in these meetings—but I still don't know what it means. Does that mean that out of the 400 calls to the abuse hotline last year you told us came from this neighborhood, there are roughly 300 or more parents who have a drug or alcohol problem? And if that is what it means, what are these projects going to do about those 300 parents—and the others that people don't make calls about? How many of them are we serving today?"

The substance abuse agency supervisor answered. "We don't have that information, but we are trying to get some of the client data for our agency geocoded for the first time so we can track clients in treatment by their neighborhoods."

"Do we know how many of them have kids?" asked the minister.

"We're trying to add that data, because in the past we didn't really see kids as part of our caseload, but now we are trying to treat the whole family. So we've added that to the intake form."

"But with all this information, how are we going to set priorities among all the projects we've proposed?" asked the vice-principal.

"First, we shouldn't just start something new unless we're sure that existing programs can't do it. And we should work harder with the programs we already have than we do setting up new ones," said the minister. "We've already agreed that the new programs should be clear about what results they are going to measure, not just tell us what they're doing or how many people they're serving."

The vice-principal asked, "What if we added a requirement that the CPS parents become a priority in treatment programs?"

The businessman asked "How do we know that treatment works? I keep hearing that treatment works, but I also hear that people keep dropping out of treatment all the time."

"How could we say that treatment works if they drop out all the time?" asked the vice-principal.

The treatment program director was looking exasperated. "What we need is a case manager who can follow up with these parents and make sure they keep coming for treatment. It isn't our fault if the clients don't show up."

Looking skeptical, the child welfare supervisor asked, "But what happens when this case manager makes the referrals? If all we're talking about is some kind of 'referral on demand,' it seems to me we haven't made much progress. Referral sure isn't treatment. We can make referrals today, and so can the judge—but all that means is that a worker gives phone numbers to some mom who has just been threatened with losing her kids. The question is—what is going to happen over at the treatment agency that is any different?"

"Remember, we haven't got any new money for these parents, and we've got other mandated priority groups," said the treatment agency director.

"How many of the welfare parents are in the CPS system?" asked the vice-principal.

The child welfare supervisor answered, "CPS clients are a small percent of all welfare parents, but the percent of CPS parents on welfare is much higher. The question is whether welfare parents who are in CPS and who volunteer for treatment should be given a priority for these new funds."

The city staff person said, "We also need to remember that there are new funds for several of these programs. The federal government has proposed new support services funding for welfare clients, the treatment block grant is getting more money, and the state is asking for a waiver so they could use child welfare funds for treatment. But we need to go after these funds right away if we are going to. There's a short window of opportunity for these new funds, and we need a new policy commitment from the city and county that they are going to go after these funds."

The minister said, "So if we've got new funding, and we're going to try to strengthen the programs that are already out there, we're beginning to develop a real agenda that is a lot more than two or three new projects. I hear you," he said, turning to the treatment program director, "on the problems with parents who don't show up for treatment. And I'm ready to recommend that those parents should not be the main caretakers for their kids. But what if our neighborhood groups and some of my church members were helping you by checking to see if these parents are doing what they need to do—and providing some continuing support after they leave your program. From what I've seen, treatment is a lifetime deal, not something you finish in 30 days."

"That would help a lot," said the treatment program director. "Let's see how that would work."

The businessman asked, "How long is all this going to take? We want to get something going right away and all these negotiations for funding and new evaluation requirements sound like they're going to take a lot of time."

"It will," said the minister. "But I'm convinced that we have to fix the system while we're trying to do a better job of serving those parents who want help and are willing to help themselves by staying in treatment."

Appendix C
Review Panel

Elaine Bush
Deputy Director
California Department Alcohol
   and Drug Programs

Steve Christian
Policy Specialist
Children & Family Program
National Council of State
   Legislators

Barbara Cimaglio
Director
Oregon Office of Alcohol and
   Drug Abuse Program

Ken DeCerchio
Assistant Secretary
Substance Abuse Program
Florida Department of Children
   and Families

Laura Feig
Social Service Analyst
Office of the Assistant Secretary
   for Planning and Evaluation
Department of Health and Human
   Services

Douglas M. Fountain
Senior Manager
The Lewin Group

Jolie Kapelus
Associate
Children's Program
Edna McConnell Clark Foundation

Naga Kasavabada
Staff Research Assistant
UCLA Drug Abuse Research Center

Marjorie Kelly
Deputy Director
CA Department of Social Services

Jill Kinney
Executive Director
Home, Safe

Guy Howard Klopp
Special Projects Consultant
Sacramento County Bureau of
   Alcohol and Drug Programs

Jacquelyn McCroskey
Associate Professor
USC School of Social Work

Toni J. Moore
Alcohol & Drug Administrator
Sacramento County
Department of Health and Human
   Services

Janice Nittoli
Senior Associate
Annie E. Casey Foundation

Susan Notkin
Director, Program for Children
Edna McConnell Clark Foundation

Ellen Shields-Fletcher
Program Manager
Training & Technical Assistance
Office of Juvenile Justice and
    Delinquency Prevention

Jeanne Reid
Senior Research Associate
National Center on Addiction &
    Substance Abuse at Columbia
    University

This guidebook was greatly improved by the valuable comments from each member of the review panel and the editing assistance of Brian Perrochet. However, the views expressed are those of the authors alone and do not reflect endorsement from the panel members or their organizations.

Appendix D
CWLA Chemical Dependency and Child Welfare Task Force

Essa Abed*
Director
Graham-Windham Services

Steve Ambrose*
Director Research and
    Demonstration Programs
Children's Institute International

Beverly Sanders Brooks
Executive Director
The Center for Children & Families

Lynda Brown*
Program Director
Progressive Life Center, Inc.

Tamara Cadet*
Technical Assistance Coordinator
Join Together

William Caltrider*
President
Center for Alcohol and Drug
Research and Education

Bruce Campbell*
Senior Staff Analyst, Department of
    Social Services
Monterey County Family and
    Children Service

Farrell Cooper
Executive Director
Family and Children's Services of
Chattanooga, Inc.

Sandra Davis-Rose
Executive Director
Cabrini Green Youth and Family
    Services

Kevin Drollinger
Executive Director
United Methodist Children and
    Family Services of Missouri

Mary Emmons*
Executive Director
Children's Institute International

Donna L.Fernandez*
Children's Services Administrator
Los Angeles Department of Children
    and Family Services

Hal Gibber
Executive Director
Tri-County Youth Programs

Fatima Goldman
Executive Director
Brookwood Child Care

Mark Hinderlie
Executive Director
Boston Children's Service

John Horngren*
Program Director
Ryther Child Center

Frances Hume*
Executive Director
Ryther Child Center

Bob Kirkman*
Program Director
Berkshire Farm Center & Services
    for Youth

Luis Medina*+
Executive Director
St. Christopher's–Jennie Clarkson
    Child Care Services, Inc.

Eleanor Mefford*
Director of Children's Services
Women In Need

John de Miranda*
Vice President of Program Services
Just Say No

Jim Mooney*
Executive Director
Metro-Dade County
Department of Youth & Family
    Development

Craig Neuman
Executive Director
Trumbull County Children Services

Angele Parker
Executive Director
Youth Continuum

Susan Penderzoli
Assistant Commissioner
Boston Department of Social
    Services

Nancy Pia
Executive Director
Project R.A.P.

Mary Redd
Executive Director
Steinway Child & Family Services

David Sanders
Director
Hennipen County Children &
    Family Services Department

Karen Selman*
Regional Executive Director
Children's Home & Aid Society of
    Illinois

David Stout*
Executive Director
Children & Family Services of Iowa

Don Thomas
Director
Hamilton County Department of
    Human Services

Kay Dean Toran*+
Director
Oregon State Office for Services to
    Children & Families

*Maxine Tucker**
Deputy Commissioner, Children &
    Youth Division
Philadelphia Department of Human
    Services

Victoria Wagner
Executive Director
YouthCare

*Sis Wenger**
Executive Director
National Association for Children of
    Alcoholics

*Gina Wood**
Director, Concentration of Federal
    Efforts Program
Washington D.C. Office of Juvenile
    Justice and Delinquency Prevention

*Katherine Wingfield**
Program Manager
Child Welfare League of America

*Pam Day**
*Michael Petit**
CWLA Staff

* Participated as a reviewer of the CWLA Guidebook
*⁺ Co-Chairs of CWLA Chemical Dependency and Child Welfare Task
    Force*

About the Authors

Nancy Young serves as Director of Children and Family Futures. She is a graduate of California State University, Fullerton, and received her M.S.W. and Ph.D. from the University of Southern California School of Social Work. She was Predoctoral Fellow with the National Institute on Drug Abuse, served as Research Consultant to the Directorate of the California Department of Alcohol and Drug Programs, and has published numerous articles on the effects of substance abuse on children and families. Dr. Young, who is married to Mr. Gardner, has a son aged 15, and she and Mr. Gardner adopted a brother and sister who arre 5 and 6 years old.

Sid Gardner serves as President of Children and Family Futures. In addition, since 1991 he has been Director of the Center for Collaboration for Children at California State University, Fullerton, a unit that seeks to train and educate professionals to be able to work across systems and to help communities involved in services integration. He is the author of a forthcoming book to be published by Arizona State University, *Beyond Collaboration to Results*. Mr. Gardner, who is married to Dr. Young, graduated from Occidental College and earned his Master's degrees from the Woodrow Wilson School at Princeton University and from Hartford Seminary. In addition to the children mentioned above, he has a 27-year-old daughter.

Kimberly Dennis is a graduate of the University of California at Berkeley and received her M.P.A. from Columbia University. After spending several years working in Washington, DC, she joined Children and Family Futures as an Associate in 1997. She is assisting with an Edna McConnell Clark Foundation grant for work in four national sites on creating partnerships for the protection of children, and a Stuart Foundation initiative in which Children and Family Futures is working to address California state and county policies concerning CWS-AOD issues.